The Democratic Trend Phenomenon

"The Predictability of the
Democratic Popular Vote for President"

Anthony E. Fairfax

The Democratic Trend Phenomenon
The Predictability of the Democratic Popular Vote for President

International Standard Book Number: 978-0-9752546-2-2

Library of Congress Control Number: 2008906414

First Printing: October 2008

Version 2

CONTENTS

LIST OF FIGURES

vi

LIST OF TABLES

DEDICATION

To my extraordinary family and friends.

Tony

ACKNOWLEDGEMENTS

Rarely do I get an opportunity to thank those who have helped me along the long road that ultimately led to developing this book. Therefore, I thought that I would take this opportunity to thank a partial list of the people who have assisted me to the place I am today. First, special thanks and love to my wife, Colita, for her enormous support during the creation of this book and other projects. Tremendous love and appreciation goes to my mother and brother, Mrs. Helen Fairfax and Rick Fairfax, for their steadfast devotion throughout my life. Adoring thoughts are sent to my daughters, Layla and Natalie. They remain motivating forces in my life to succeed. And, to my father, who will always be remembered as an officer and a gentleman.

I would also like to say thanks: To my small group of first cousins, Leslie, Steve, Stephanie, Reah, Eric, and my wonderful aunts and uncles, both who have past and survived. Thanks for those little enjoyable moments growing up; To my beautiful cousin Monique and our friend Janet, thanks for introducing me to some neat media folk; To my oldest buddies J and Mike whom I have known for a lifetime. J, thanks for teaming with me on all of our business projects; To the fellas who got me through college at Tech: Burn, D, Irv, Joe, J Smith, and O (who are also known as the Copas). I probably would not have a college degree without you guys (or was it that I almost did not get a degree because of you guys). G, you joined the group late, but, you are included as well; To SHT, thanks for giving it a try with the training center; To Winnett at DS and Rudy at NSU, thanks for some very interesting and challenging work that literally changed my life.

Finally, I would like to thank those who were part of the organization that I was working for when I discovered the Trend, the CBC Institute. Thanks Janice, Art, Andrea, Marsha, Alicia and the Board (and thanks for the recommendation, Anita). Congressmen Clyburn, Hilliard, Kilpatrick, C. Meek, Thompson, and of course Watt, thanks for solidified my faith in our country's legislative system.

All of these individuals in some small or large way contributed to my growth as a person and thus ultimately to this book. I thank you all.

ABOUT THE AUTHOR

Mr. Fairfax began his career working as a Hardware Design Engineer for Teledyne Inc. and then for Engineering and Economic Research (EER) Systems. However, for over a decade and a half, Mr. Fairfax has worked as a demographic data/mapping consultant. As a consultant he has been contracted to provide support to a variety of public and private organizations. Fairfax's consulting work experience began in 1991 with Norfolk State University's Redistricting Research Project. Throughout the next decade, he personally developed over 300 redistricting plans for jurisdictions as small as cities and towns to areas as large as congressional districts. In addition, Mr. Fairfax provided technical services as a non-testifying expert for three court cases including a renowned redistricting Supreme Court case.

In 2001, ten years after he began providing demographic/mapping services, he was selected to be the Demographer for the newly founded Congressional Black Caucus Political Education and Leadership Institute (CBC Institute) located in Washington, D.C. For a span of two years Mr. Fairfax provided consulting services for the Redistricting Project that developed and analyzed over 75 congressional plans in 15 different states.

In 2004, Mr. Fairfax began providing a variety of project related services as Democracy South's (DS) Senior Technical Consultant. Project efforts have centered on voter data analysis and targeting. He also supported various DS clients such as multiple USAction state partners. He also provided critical support for two distinct projects: *Voter Contact Magazine* (Associate Editor) and the Missing Voter Project (Co-Director). *Voter Contact Magazine* is a new publication that contains useful and critical information for voter engagement personnel. The Missing Voter Project is a voter registration and voter mobilization program that utilizes voter data, targeting technology, and mapping to locate then reach out to individuals who are not registered as well as those voters who have a propensity to not vote.

Throughout the years he has co-founded and owned several small businesses, including: a mapping firm (GeoTek); one of first Internet Video search guides (MediaChannel.com); a digital signage business (AdCast Inc); and his demographic consulting business (CensusChannel).

Exemplifying his expertise, Mr. Fairfax published a unique book on accessing and utilizing Census data: *A Step-by-Step Guide to Using Census 2000 Data* (2004). He holds a Bachelor of Science degree in Electrical Engineering from Virginia Tech. Fairfax resides in Hampton, Virginia, is married to Dr. Colita Nichols Fairfax, and has two daughters, Layla and Natalie.

PREFACE

Theories of political realignments have been around for decades. Most of these theories involved a shifting of political power from one party to another. In addition, these realignment theories, in some cases, enabled accurately projecting the "winner" of a particular election but not an accurate projection of the popular vote. The central reason was that regardless of the realignment, forecasting the popular vote, with a high degree of accuracy, was extremely difficult due to different national or even local conditions as well as diverse candidates that change with each election.

However, for almost three decades our country's electorate exhibited the effects from a major political realignment. The consequence of this realignment was a little known or possibly unknown phenomenon pertaining to the popular vote for president. The phenomenon was that the popular vote for the Democratic candidate for president trended in a predictable pattern from 1972 to 2000 (if the election of 1976 is disregarded). In fact, the Trend was so predictable that the popular vote for the Democratic candidates, in the elections of 1992, 1996, and 2000, could have *all* been determined in 1988 with an accuracy of 99% or better.

This extraordinary predictability has been deemed by this author as, *"The Democratic Trend Phenomenon."* This book describes the cause of the phenomenon, measures its predictability, and outlines the future effects.

Amazingly, the predictable Trend occurred despite the fact that each election contained varying turnout percentages, different U.S. and global conditions, different opponents, and diverse candidates. The latter declarations may be extremely intriguing and most likely controversial when you consider the Republican candidates range from Richard Nixon to Ronald Reagan to George W. Bush and the Democratic candidates ranged from George McGovern to Bill Clinton to John Kerry.

The structure of this book is divided into four (4) distinct sections. Those who are statistically challenged, but desire to obtain the essence of the book, may choose to read only the descriptive portions (Chapters 1-6 and 12-13). Chapter 1, "The Story of The Democratic Trend," will present the reader with a chronology of the discovery of the phenomenon and acts as a condensed version of the entire book. Nevertheless, those who wish to dust off the old stats book (or crack open a new one) may find the statistics chapters (Chapters 7-11) interesting along with the data supplied in the Appendices.

Part One of the book includes chapters that describe the phenomenon as well as discuss the historical environment that existed in order to create the predictable Trend itself. Part Two includes chapters with statistical techniques that prove the presence of the Phenomenon and other observable theories. Part Three analyzes the phenomenon at the state level. Part Four includes chapters that outline the future potential results regarding the popular vote for the candidates running for president.

It is important to note that this book discusses the Democratic Trend that occurs at the Presidential level. It does not address any phenomenon that may occur for any other political office. As a result, the purpose of this book is to present and discuss a unique and possibly unknown phenomenon pertaining to the popular vote for the Democratic candidate for president.

PART 1

The Phenomenon

The Democratic Trend Phenomenon

Chapter 1

The Story of the Democratic Trend

Introduction

President Lyndon B. Johnson leaned over and remarked to his press secretary, who was Bill Moyers at the time, *"I think we have just delivered the South to the Republican Party for a long time to come."*[1] This "legendary" statement, which many political analysts now feel rang true, would resonate with me when I began to write this book. For those of you who are familiar with the quote, you will understand the context of his statement. For those who are not familiar, continue to read and you will soon discover the meaning and its association with this book.

Years ago, when I first read President Johnson's quote, the words did not resonate with me until the day a unique phenomenon was discovered. On that day of discovery I was sitting at my desk in Washington D.C. reviewing a series of reports. At the time I was consulting on a project for a newly formed nonprofit organization.[2] I was hired to be the demographer for a redistricting project.

During that period of time I was analyzing U.S. Census Bureau documents describing the results of the Census 2000 survey. For some reason I continued to glance back at a particular graph. The graph depicted the votes cast, or in other words the popular vote for president, by a major political party from 1972 to 2000. I had seen this graph before, or at least a similar one, but had never seen the pattern that was discovered on that day.

---

[1] New York Times, *Divisive Words: News Analysis; G.O.P.'S 40 Years Of Juggling On Race* 2002, Adam Clymer.
[2] The official name of the organization was the Congressional Black Caucus Political Education and Leadership Institute or CBC Institute.

Take an opportunity to glance at a copy of the graph located in Figure 1-1 and see if you can pick out the pattern. Did you recognize the pattern? Was it obvious to you? If you did not see the pattern, look at the following page to view a recreation of the same graph with votes cast for the Republican and Other Major candidates removed (see Figure 1-2).

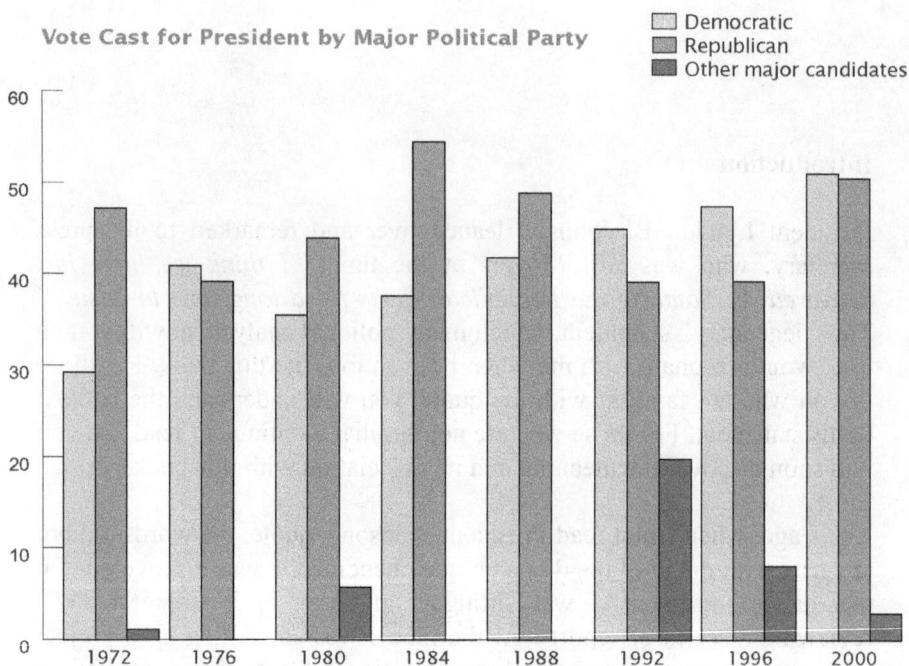

Source: U.S. Census Bureau, Statistical Abstract of the United States: 2001

Figure 1-1 - Votes Cast for President by Major Party
(1972 to 2000)

As you can clearly see, the popular vote for the Democratic candidate follows a straight line, or in more technical terms displays a "linear" trend from 1980 to 2000. Once the Trend was revealed to me, I immediately saw it every time that I glanced back at the graph. If you are wondering just how "linear" the Trend is, make sure that you read Chapter 7. In Chapter 7 statistical regression was applied to determine how closely the Trend follows a straight line. In fact, I later discovered that the Trend was so straight and predictable that the popular vote for

4

the Democratic candidates, in the elections of 1992, 1996, and 2000, could have been determined in 1988 with an accuracy of 99% or better (see Chapter 8).

Popular Vote for Democratic Presidential Candidates (1972 - 2000)

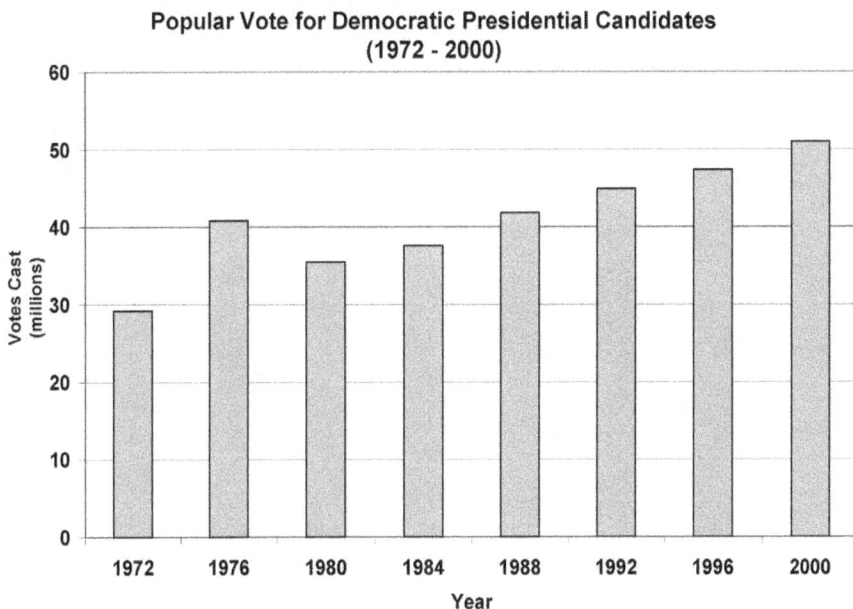

Source: U.S. Census Bureau, Statistical Abstract of the United States: 2001

Figure 1-2 - Popular Vote for Democratic Presidential Candidates (1972 to 2000)

In some circumstances a linear trend may not be an oddity. In fact, in many cases we expect to see a linear trend. Most of us have seen linear trends in graphs that depict population growth. However, when I viewed the Republican popular vote over the same period of time, it seemingly showed no visible pattern at all (see Figure 1-3). I say "seemingly" because I discovered later that there was a second more obscure pattern pertaining to the Republican and Other candidates as well (see Chapter 4). To reiterate, at first it may seem to some that the Democratic linear trend should be the normal trend and the Republican "fluctuating" may be the oddity. This stance can be quickly overturned when you realize that each presidential election had different turnout percentages of the popular vote that "should" have garnered fluctuating popular vote for each candidate from election to election.

Popular Vote for Republican Presidential Candidates (1972 - 2000)

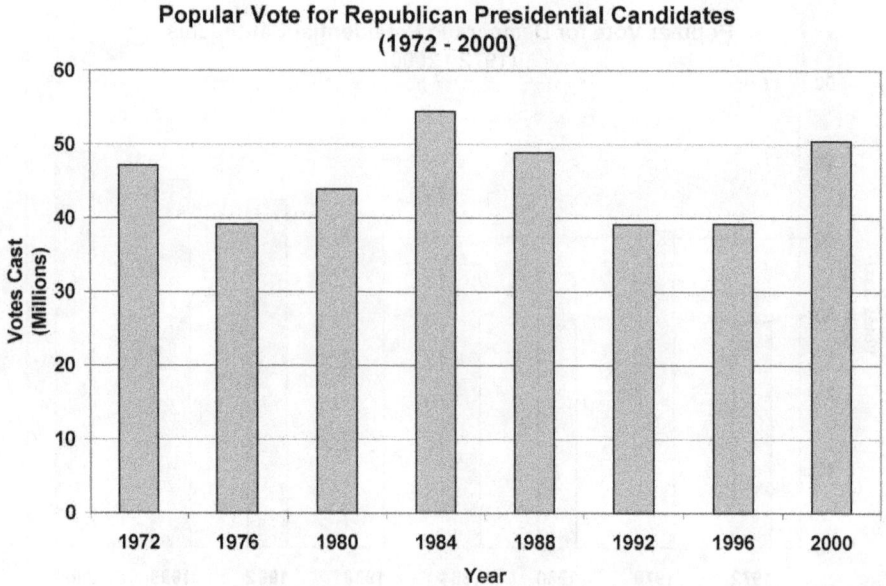

Source: U.S. Census Bureau, Statistical Abstract of the United States: 2001

Figure 1-3 - Popular Vote for Republican Presidential Candidates (1972 to 2000)

To illustrate this difference, look at Figure 1-4 and review the varying turnout percentages for the presidential elections from 1980 to 2000. In order for the growth of the votes cast to increase in a straight line there should be a consistent turnout percentage or at least a steadily increasing or even decreasing pattern.

As Figure 1-4 indicates, there seems to be no consistent linear pattern for the turnout percentage. The graph shows that in some elections there was an increase in the turnout from the previous election, in others there was a decrease. This makes perfect sense when considering the fact that a variety of different Republican and Democratic candidates, each with differing appeal, should garner different voter turnout. Consider the Republican candidates: Ronald Reagan, George H.W. Bush, Bob Dole, and George W. Bush. Now consider the Democratic candidates: Jimmy

Carter, Walter Mondale, Michael Dukakis, Bill Clinton, and Al Gore. You can easily see that they represented different characteristics and thus should garner differing popular votes.

Voter Turnout as a Percentage of Voting Age Population (1980 - 2000)

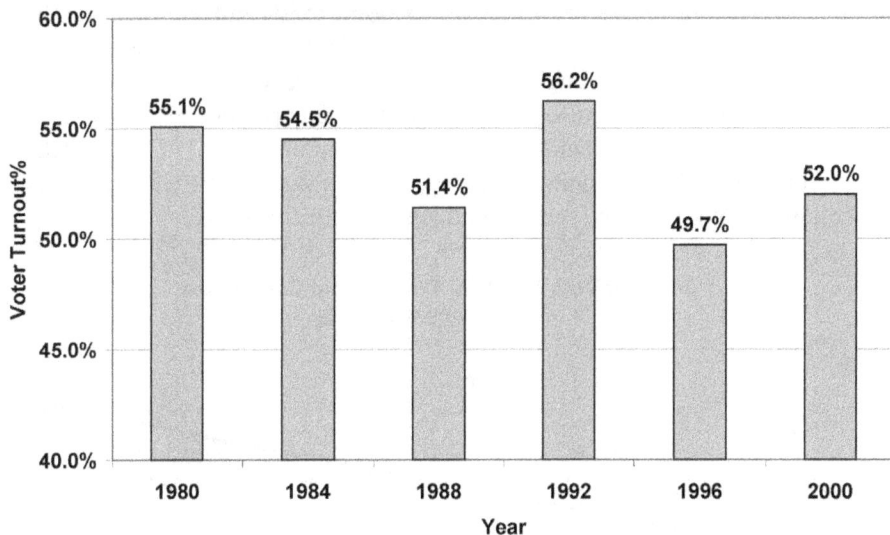

Source: U.S. Census Bureau Statistical Abstract of the U.S., 2004 (Table HS-52)

Figure 1-4 - Voter Turnout as a Percentage of Voting Age Population (1980 to 2000)

It was observed that the Republican candidates' popular vote varied, the overall turnout varied, but the Democratic candidate's votes consistently trended upward. Clearly, the oddity was the linear trend of the Democratic candidates and not the varying votes for the Republican candidates. This discrepancy was baffling. How could a linear trend exist when the turnout of all voters as well as candidates varied from election to election?

Nevertheless, before solving that question, it was observed that the Democratic Trend from 1980 to 2000 seemed to align itself with the election of 1972. At the same time, it did not line up with the 1976 election. To view the Trend without obstruction, a new graph was developed that displayed the Trend from 1972 to 2000 with the 1976 election removed (see Figure 1-5).

The fact that the 1976 election was not aligned with the other elections did not deter me from viewing the Trend as linear. Rationale for this line of thinking was that in the world of statistics there is a term known as "outlier." An outlier occurs when a data point exists outside the overall pattern of distribution. For those that find that statement pure jabberwocky, I am speaking of the well-known "exception to the rule." Outliers are commonly discarded when analyzing a trend pattern. This did not mean that I did not question what occurred in 1976. In fact, Chapter 3 details my synopsis of the 1976 election. However, 1976 election was not included in the trend analysis for this book.

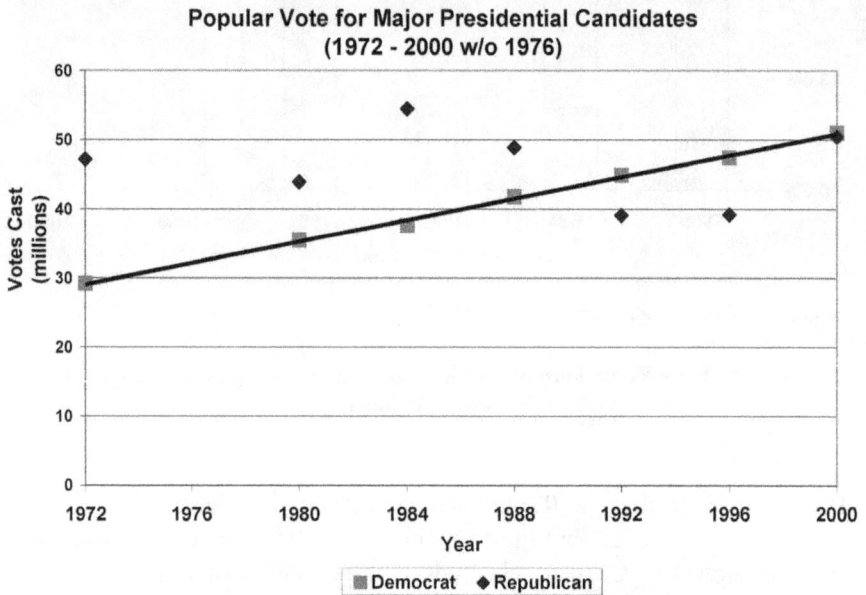

Popular Vote for Major Presidential Candidates (1972 - 2000 w/o 1976)

Source: U.S. Census Bureau, Statistical Abstract of the United States: 2001

Figure 1-5 - Popular Vote for Major Presidential Candidates
(1972 to 2000 w/o 1976)

Figure 1-5 epitomized the uniqueness of the Trend. That is to say that the Democratic popular vote increased in a linear fashion while the Republican vote fluctuates. Within a relatively short period of time after discovering the Trend, there were several questions that needed to be answered, including:

1. When did the Trend begin?
2. What caused the Trend to be linear?
3. What created the Trend?
4. Were there other associated trends?
5. What occurred in 1976?
6. How does 2004 align with the Trend?
7. Is the Trend a phenomenon or phenomena?
8. What does the future hold for the Trend?

When Did The Trend Begin?

In order to unravel the genesis of the Democratic Trend there needed to be a determination of when the Trend began. Did the Trend begin in 1972 or did it begin prior to that time?

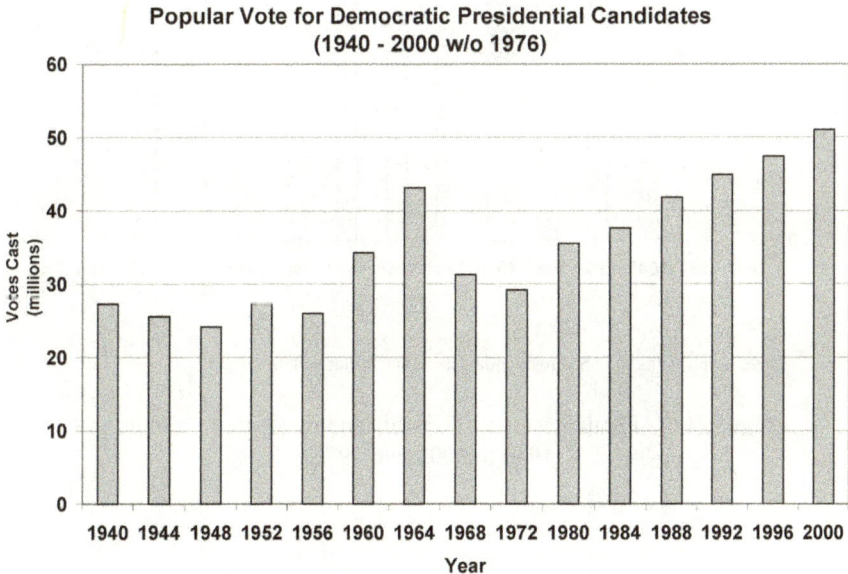

Popular Vote for Democratic Presidential Candidates (1940 - 2000 w/o 1976)

Source: Dave Leip's Atlas of U.S. Presidential Elections, uselectionatlas.org

Figure 1-6 - Popular Vote for Democratic Presidential Candidates (1940 to 2000 w/o 1976)

The first step was to obtain the election results prior 1972. I turned to one of the best "all-in-one" website locations for past presidential, senatorial, and gubernatorial election results, "Dave Leip's Atlas of U.S. Presidential Elections" located at uselectionatlas.org. Leip has spent years collecting election results from official sources to create an expansive repository[3].

Using the data obtained from Leip, a new graph was created that showed the popular vote for the Democratic candidates from 1940 to 2000 (see Figure 1-6). There was no visible indication of a linear trend prior to 1972.

**Popular Vote for Republican Presidential Candidates
(1940 - 2000 w/o 1976)**

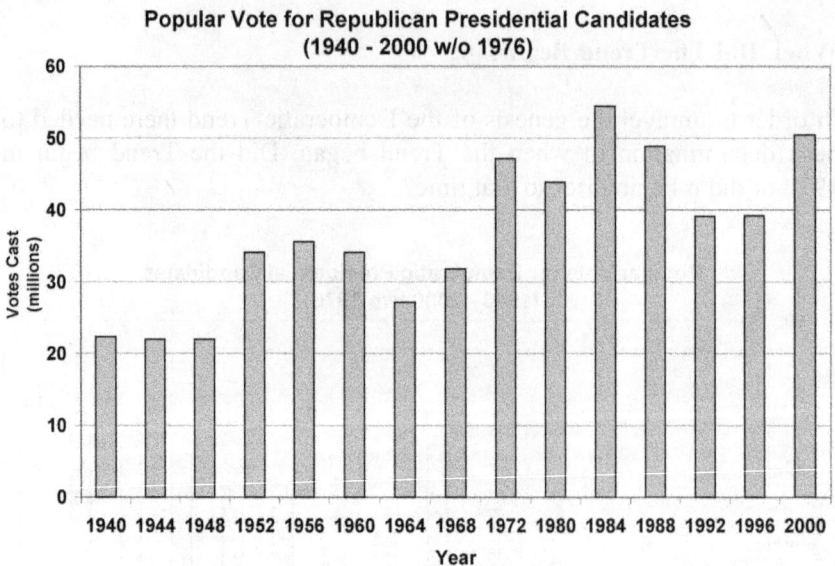

Source: Dave Leip's Atlas of U.S. Presidential Elections, uselectionatlas.org

Figure 1-7 - Popular Vote for Republican Presidential Candidates
(1940 to 2000 w/o 1976)

---

[3] Although I discovered various other sources for the popular vote for president, that had data values that differed slightly from Leip's website, the differences amounted to less than a fraction of one percent.

Just for comparison sake, a graph of the Republican candidate's popular vote from 1940 to 2000 was created (see Figure 1-7). Once again there was no visible consistent linear trend.[4]

To ensure that the votes cast were not linear, linear regression was used to determine how closely the popular vote followed a straight line. The numerical results gave no indication of a linear trend for the Democratic or Republican candidates (see Chapter 3).

Therefore, the first question had been solved. The Trend seemed to begin in 1972. Now, on to solving the "Cause of the Trend."

What Caused The Trend To Be Linear?

The central underlining question of this theory was, "What would cause the popular vote for the Democratic candidate to be linear?" Of course, this requires an initial assumption that a trend such as this would not occur naturally. There had to be some unique circumstance for the popular vote of the Democratic candidates to align itself in a straight line while the popular vote for the Republican candidate varied from election to election. There was one additional assumption. The other assumption was that something "substantial" must have occurred during or prior to the 1972 election in order for the linear trend to begin.

As I went through various scenarios of how the popular vote would increase in a steadily predictable pattern, I came across a previously created graph that gave me a clue (see Figure 1-8). The graph depicted the increase in voting age population (VAP) from 1972 to 2000 elections. The voting age population includes those persons who are above the age of 18 years old.[5]

The graph of the VAP was so similar to the graph of the popular vote for the Democratic candidate that I contemplated that there was a connection between the two. The connection was that the linear Democratic Trend was related to the increase in VAP. To some this may seem like an easy connection to make. You may be thinking, "of course it is the increase in

---

[4] There was a peculiar voting consistency for 1940, 1944, and 1948 for the Republican candidate that should be researched later.
[5] Prior to 1972 some states minimum voting age was older than 21 years or even more.

11

population." Again, the caveat was that it *only* showed the increase in population. The emphasis is on the "only." This means that just about every other factor had *not* impacted the vote for the Democratic candidate - except the increase in population.[6] This included factors such as: different election turnout percentages, candidates, current domestic or global conditions, and just about any other aspect that you can think of, did not impact the votes cast for the Democratic candidate.

**Voting Age Population in Presidential Elections
(1972 - 2000)**

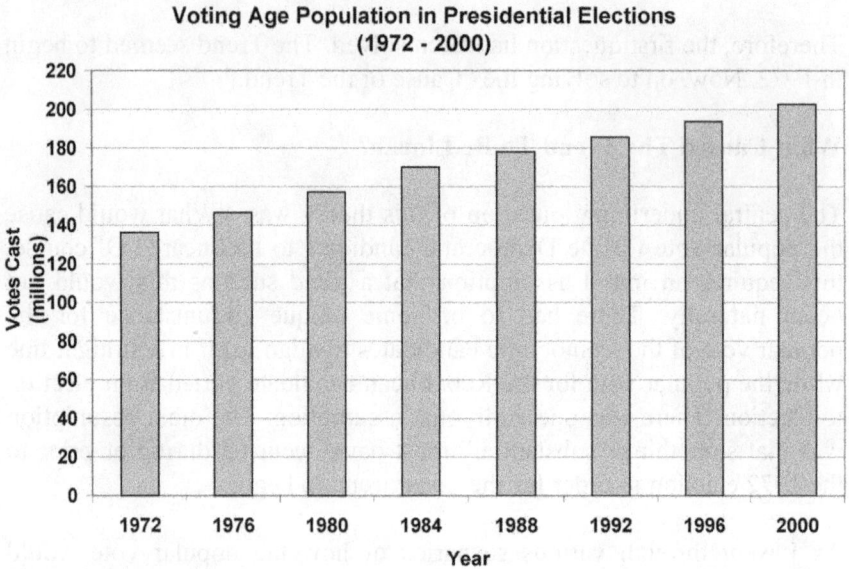

Source: U.S. Census Bureau, Reported Voting Rates in Presidential Election Years, by Selected Characteristics: November 1964 to 2004

Figure 1-8 - Voting Age Population in Presidential Elections
(1972 to 2000)

Without dwelling on how astounding that last statement was, the question momentarily shifted from "What caused the Trend to be linear?" to "Why did the votes cast for the Democratic candidate only include the increase in population?" Posed with the latter question, there could only be one answer - the same groups of voters are voting for the

---

[6] To demonstrate how well the Democratic votes cast related to the overall VAP from 1972 to 2000 (excluding 1976), the ratio of the Democratic popular vote to VAP varied from 21.4% to 25.2% while the Republican popular vote to VAP varied from 20.2% to 34.6%.

Democratic candidate in each election. In essence, there had to be a particular type of voter that always voted for the Democratic candidate and consequently the Trend was following the increase in population of that group.

So, the third sub-question in this linear trend mystery becomes "What group of voters always vote for the Democratic candidate?" This question was straightforward and one that was relatively easy to answer. The group of voters that always vote for the Democratic candidate are the "Democratic base voters." Base voters are those voters who are predisposed to always vote for their party's candidate.[7] Not only that, for this unique case, these base voters seem to always vote. These important characteristics led me to believe that these were not the ordinary base voters that are normally spoken about, but were instead what I labeled as the "core" base voters.

At this point I need to state one vital stipulation. These core base voters, who formed the Democratic Trend, do so in "presidential elections." For the purpose of this book I did not research and have not discovered a similar trend related to other types of political offices (congressional, gubernatorial, etc.). In other words, these unique voters form a trend when voting in presidential elections "only." I found no indication and have not analyzed the core base voters or the Trend in other offices above and beyond presidential.[8]

Again, as previously stated, I came to realize that these Democratic voters always or most always voted. Simply put, if they did not vote all or most of the time, the trend would *not* have been linear. The popular vote for the Democratic candidate would have trended similarly to the popular vote for the Republican candidate. It would have fluctuated with the turnout of voters. It did not.

Once that last question was answered, the original question was answered. The answer was that the Democratic Trend was actually the increase in core Democratic base voters. The popular vote of the

---

[7] Jody C. Baumgartner, Peter L. Francia, *Conventional Wisdom and American Elections*, Rowman & Littlefield, pg 207

[8] Even with the core base voters there is always a small percentage that do not conform to the Democratic Trend. Nonetheless, this seems to be less than 6% from 1972 to 2004 with the major exception of the election of 1976.

Democratic candidate included only or mostly these core base voters. This was the central reason why the popular vote for the Democratic candidate deviated very little from election to election. The popular vote only reflected a steady increase proportionate to the increase in population. Hence, after 1972 the popular vote for Democratic candidate for president was linear and almost entirely made up of Democratic base voters.

This discovery of the cause of the linear trend opened the door to solve the most important question of all, "What created the Trend?"

What Created the Trend?

Out of all of the questions centering on the Democratic Trend Phenomenon, the most critical one of them all was, "What created the Trend?" This question had been nagging me from the beginning. However, I had to answer the previous questions in order to be capable of answering this fundamental one. In effect, I had several components of this analytical puzzle in place with one big hole in the middle. The pieces that had been found included:

1. There was no visible indication of the Trend from 1940 to 1972;
2. The linear trend of the Democratic popular vote began in 1972 and continued to at least the year 2000 (excluding 1976);
3. The Democratic popular vote after 1972 was essentially made up of the core Democratic base voters who always or mostly voted for the Democratic candidate, thus, created the linearity;
4. These core Democratic base voters tended to always vote.

Once again, I approached solving this question by solving a simpler question. The simpler question was "Why did the Democratic popular vote only contain the base voters after 1972?" The general answer to this question was easy. Something had to occur to the electorate to cause only the base Democratic voters to vote for the Democratic candidate. Whatever occurred had to be substantial and had to affect the entire national electorate. In order to determine what occurred our electorate had to be viewed in a unique manner.

Understanding that there had been other times in our electoral history where voting behavior changed, I began researching past types of voting trends or as political scientists call them "realignments." I came across a dominating theory by Louis Bean, a political prognosticator, which centered on a particular voting trend analogy (see Chapter 3). Bean's analogy was that occasionally there were conditions in our country where one political Party comes into power like a "tidal wave" coming onto shore.[9] That Party would remain in power for a particular period of time.[10] Then, just like tidal waves that roll back out to sea, so would the Party's control. Nonetheless, the political realignment that is being described in this book was something different from the tidal wave theory. Those theories did not fully explain the linear trending phenomenon; so, I was forced to expand their theories to include this phenomenon.

At this point I began developing the theory with the assumption that after 1972 the Democratic popular vote was essentially the core Democratic base voters. Once that assumption was made, I fairly quickly realized that if these base voters had become the only voters voting for the Democratic candidate, they might as well be voting in a separate electorate. In fact, in order to understand the Democratic Trend, our presidential electorate had to be viewed not as one but as two separate electorates. As a result, it was surmised that, for all practical purposes, our presidential electorate had been "fractured" into two pieces.

The first portion of the electorate had already been established. It was the part that contained the core Democratic base voters. What was concluded was that if there was, in essence, a separate electorate that only contained voters that vote for the Democratic candidate and always vote, the result would be a linear trend. As stated previously, the reason for the linear trend was that the votes cast from election to election depicted the increase in population of the core Democratic base voters.

I titled this first part the **Democrat** electorate since it contained essentially the core Democratic base voters. Given that the voters included in the second part of the electorate, did not, or at best, hardly ever, vote for the Democratic presidential candidate, I called this part the **Non-Democrat** electorate (see Figure 1-9).

---

[9] Louis Bean, who predicted the win by Truman against Dewey in 1948, has been credited for developing the concept of "political cycles" or "political tides."

[10] Usually the realignments last between 30 to 40 years.

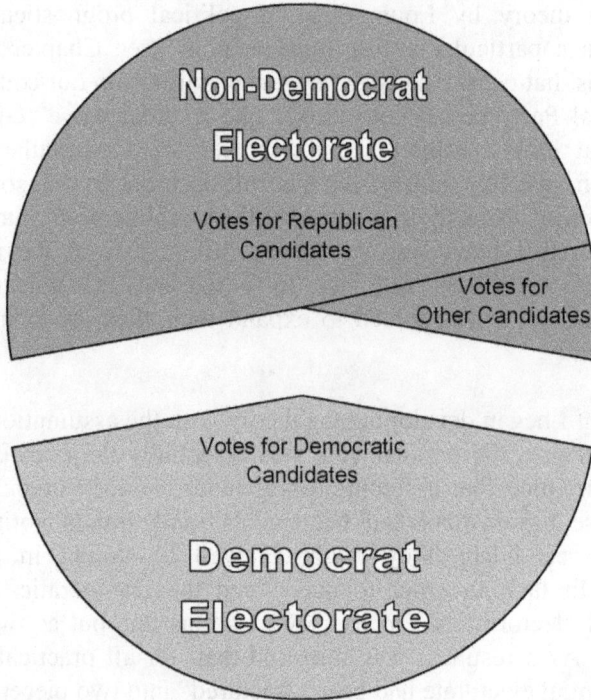

Figure 1-9 - Graphical Representation of Fractured Presidential Electorate

So, the question "Why did the Democratic candidates' popular vote only contain the base voters after 1972?" has been answered. The answer was that our voting electorate, at the presidential level, had been fractured into two pieces. One piece contained voters who voted for the Democratic candidate for president. The other piece contained the voters who voted for the Republican candidate for president in addition to the voters who voted for Non-Major Party candidates. Next, on to solving the real question of "What Caused the Trend?"

Since the linearity of the elections showed that the electorate was fractured into two pieces, focus could occur on the cause of the fracturing. Answering that question also answers the question "What caused the Trend?" Thus, my next objective was to examine what major event or events occurred around 1972 to fracture our electorate.

I could reasonably assume that something substantial had to have occurred in our country in order for a sizable part of the electorate to decide not to vote for the Democratic candidate. Substantial meant that whatever occurred seem to have affected voters nationally. This is obviously true since the Democratic candidate received votes throughout the entire country. The next assumption was that voters shifting "away" from the Democratic presidential candidates or Party due to something that they disagreed with.

Therefore, I began with the concept that the Democratic candidates or Party must have promoted or backed certain policies or achieved something that a sizable portion of the electorate disagreed with. Thus, they made a conscience decision to shift away from the Party. Those voters must have disagreed with these policies so much that this portion of the electorate would not vote for the Democratic candidate for the next 30 years or more (excluding 1976).

The natural starting point for me was the 1972 election itself. In that election, the Democratic candidate was Senator George McGovern and the Republican was President Richard Nixon who was seeking his second term. Nixon won in what would be considered a landslide. He won 49 states to McGovern's one state and the District of Columbia. McGovern's platform included a fundamental issue - ending the Vietnam War[11]. Nixon also promised that peace was nearing in Vietnam by continuing to implement his policies. Because both sides were touting that they would end the war, I surmised that the Vietnam War could not have been the major occurrence that fractured the electorate in two pieces. Vietnam may have played some type of role, just not the dominant one.

Senator McGovern was also labeled by Nixon as "too liberal for the country." Nixon reinforced a statement by Senator Thomas Eagleton that McGovern is for "Amnesty, Abortion and Acid."[12] Under normal circumstances that statement would not have been unusual. However, Eagleton just happened to be selected as McGovern's Vice Presidential candidate. Later, McGovern fired Eagleton and selected Sargent Shriver as his running mate. Nonetheless, this liberal label attached to McGovern

---

[11] McGovern also promised to institute programs that would guarantee income to the nations poor.
[12] Time Magazine, August 1972 Issue, "The Eagleton Affair."

was not enough to fracture the voting electorate and establish a trend for the next three decades. Once again, this liberal aspect of the Democratic candidate played a role in the fracturing, just not the primary one.

After reviewing the events of the 1972 election no evidence was substantial enough to fracture the electorate. As I continued to research, I recalled that the presidential election of 1968 was considered by many political analysts to be a "realigning election."[13] The election ended the dominance by the Democratic Party that began with Franklin Roosevelt in 1932.[14] In fact, an aid to Richard Nixon, Kevin P. Phillips wrote that after the 1968 election, *a realignment* occurred whereby the southern region of the country would ultimately become Republican.[15] Therefore, I contemplated, "what if the Trend began in 1972, but, the fracturing occurred prior to that time?" The events centering around the 1968 election was immediately reviewed.

What came to mind about the 1968 election was that it exemplified the decade of sixties. In fact, some called the sixties the "turbulent sixties" (see Chapter 2). Throughout the sixties there was a growing divide in the country due to several divisive issues such as: the increase in recreational drug use; a new sexual revolution; the women's liberation movement; a prolonged war in Vietnam; and of course civil rights. The unique aspect of most of these major issues in the sixties was that they were all dividing the country into "liberal" and "conservative." Excluding the war, all of the other major positions favoring these movements were considered liberal and increasingly being associated with the Democratic Party. Consequently, this growing division of our society was literally "pulling" our electorate apart. With the convolution of these divergent issues our electorate was literally stretching throughout the sixties to a breaking point. It was simply a matter of time before one of the issues became a catalyst for a major electoral realignment.

---

[13] The small debate of whether a realignment in 1968 occurred or did not occur is over. The shear existence of the Democratic Trend confirms the reality of not just a realignment, but, a "major" realignment. It was a realignment that the country has never experienced before. Regardless of whether there is agreement on the cause of the realignment, the Democratic Trend makes it undeniable that a realignment has occurred. Therefore, the debate can finally be put to rest.

[14] Franklin Roosevelt's New Deal shifted millions of Republican voters to become Democratic voters.

[15] Nicol C. Rae, *Southern Democrat*, Oxford University Press, 1994

Now, back to the election of 1968. During that year: Dr. Martin Luther King Jr. and Robert Kennedy were assassinated; race riots proliferated throughout the country; violence occurred at the 1968 Democratic convention; and there were wide spread protests against the Vietnam war. Because of these events, along with the fact that President Lyndon Johnson decided not to seek an additional term, the Democratic Party and much of the country, was left in somewhat of disarray.

Since the Democratic Party had no clear-cut succession of leadership, some scholars believe the 1968 presidential convention was divided into several factions[16]:

1) *Big-city party bosses, led by Mayor Richard J. Daily of Chicago, IL. This faction supported Senator Hubert Humphrey;*

2) *Followers of Senator Eugene McCarthy who were comprised mostly of activist against the Vietnam War;*

3) *Catholics, African Americans, and other racial and ethnic minorities. These individuals were rallying behind Senator Robert Kennedy; and*

4) *White Southern Democrats or "Dixiecrats." Some of these members supported Hubert Humphrey; however, most of them would end up supporting George C. Wallace from Alabama.*

The particular faction that stood out to me was the fourth group that consisted mostly of white Southern Democrats. As you probably recall, Alabama's George C. Wallace, **"broke-off"**[17] from the Democratic Party to lead the charge to join and expand the American Independent Party. George Wallace received over 9.9 million votes or 13.5% of the popular vote. This was the largest third Party vote total since 1924.[18]

---

[16] Phillip E. Converse, Warren E. Miller, Jerrold G. Rusk, Arthur C. Wolfe, *Continuity and Change in American Politics: Parties and Issues in the 1968 Election,* 1969; Wikipedia, *United States Presidential Election, 1968*

[17] I later found out that the term "broke-off" was a perfect description for what occurred.

[18] In 1924, Republican Robert M. La Follette received 4,831,706 votes for 16.6% of the popular vote.

As most will recall several years before, in 1962, Wallace was elected governor of Alabama on a pro-segregation, pro-states' rights platform. He won a landslide victory. At that time he gave his most infamous speech that included:

> "In the name of the greatest people that have ever trod
> this earth, I draw the line in the dust and toss the gauntlet
> before the feet of tyranny, and I say segregation now,
> segregation tomorrow, segregation forever."

In 1963, Wallace made news again by standing in front of an auditorium at the University of Alabama in order to stop two black students, Vivian Malone and James Hood from enrolling. Using his public image, Wallace ran, albeit unsuccessfully, for the "Democratic" nomination for president in 1964. In the 1968 election his prior words and track record still resonated with some of the voters. Wallace and the American Independent Party vehemently opposed the 1964 Civil Rights Act. It was not that they simply opposed the 1964 Civil Rights Act, they opposed federal efforts to end desegregation including opposition to the 1965 Voting Rights Act and the 1968 Civil Rights Act (also known as the Fair Housing Act). The Civil Rights Act of 1964 prohibited discrimination in public facilities and certain employment practices; the Voting Rights Act of 1965 prohibited discriminatory practices in voting, and the Civil Rights Act of 1968 outlawed discrimination in the sale or rental of housing.

The statement that President Johnson made to his press secretary after signing the Civil Rights Act needs to be repeated. He stated, *"I think we have just delivered the South to the Republican Party for a long time to come."* Johnson instinctively felt that a portion of the country, specifically the South, was not ready for the change that was about to occur due to civil rights legislation. He knew that although polls indicated a majority of the country favored the Civil Rights Act, there was a part of the country that adamantly opposed it. For instance, 62% of those surveyed in the Harris Poll of April 1964 stated that they favored such a law. Similar finding were made regarding the Voting Rights Act. A Gallup poll taken in the spring of 1965 showed that 75% favored federal voting rights legislation[19]. However, how adamant were those that did not support the legislation? A better question was, "did a portion

---

[19] Isserman, Maurice & Kazin, Michael. *America Divided*, pg 142

of the population feel that the country was moving too fast with civil rights legislation?

Case in point, another Gallup poll in 1965 showed that 42% of the population indicated that the government was moving too fast in implementing voting rights legislation.[20] Although the implications of the 1965 Gallup poll was fascinating, the polling preceding the 1968 Fair Housing Act was much more revealing. In 1967, a Gallup poll declared that between 1963 and 1965, 69% to 71% of "Whites" said that they might move or would move if a great number of "Negroes" moved into the neighborhood.[21]

What was becoming clear was that after two prior seminal civil rights acts, the 1968 Fair Housing Act, was what I determined to be the proverbial "last straw" for a certain segment of the population. Furthermore, as a direct beneficiary, George Wallace garnered the support of millions of voters who were disgruntled with the direction of the country regarding civil rights policies. More importantly, these policies were perceived by the general population to be championed by the Democratic Party.

Once I realized that Wallace obtained a substantial amount of voters who were disillusioned with the path that the Democratic Party was taking regarding to civil rights, and were being tied to "liberal" issues, I decided to add the 1968 election to the previous trend graph. The popular vote for 1968 election along with the popular vote for the presidential elections from 1972 through 2000 were compared (see Figure 1-10).

What was apparent was that the 1968 Democratic popular vote was approximately the same amount as the 1972 election. Returning to my original idea, I surmised that the fracturing of our electorate occurred in 1968 by many of the Wallace voters **"breaking off"** from voting for the Democratic candidate for president. When this fracturing occurred it left only the core Democratic base voters voting for the Democratic candidate.

---

[20] Gallup, George & Gallup Jr., Alec. *The Gallup Poll 1999*, 2000, pg 237
[21] Christopher Bonastia , *Knocking on the Door: The Federal Government's Attempt to Desegregate*, pg 88, Princeton University Press, 2006

**Popular Vote for Democratic Presidential Candidates
(1968 - 2000)**

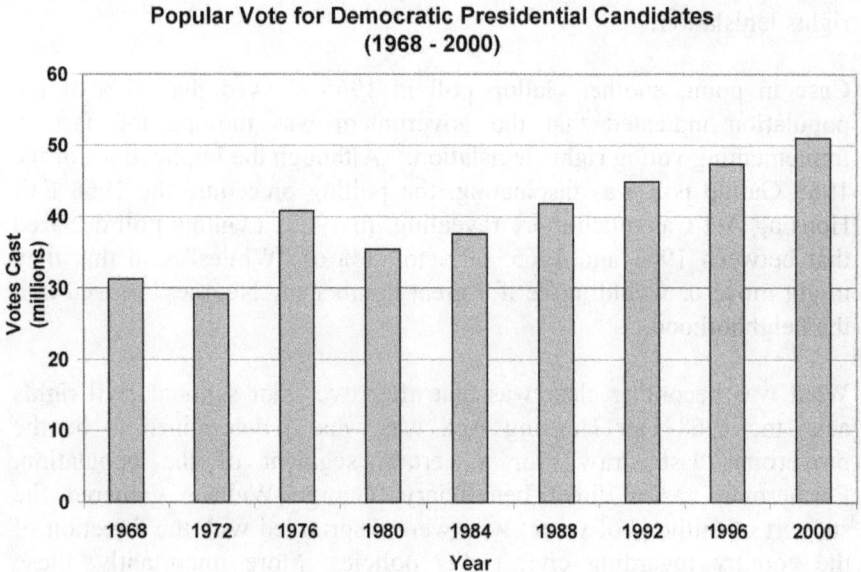

Source: Dave Leip's Atlas of U.S. Presidential Elections, uselectionatlas.org

Figure 1-10 - 1968 to 2000 Democratic Popular Vote

Nonetheless, Senator Hubert Humphrey, the Democratic candidate in 1968, garnered more votes than Senator George McGovern in 1972. What occurred was that the fracturing was not complete. In 1968, a small amount of Humphrey's voters did not break off and instead continued to vote for the Democratic candidate. However, in the election of 1972 these voters ultimately dropped off leaving only the core Democratic base voters.

It is important to note that this fracturing might not have occurred if it were not for the other divisions in the country previously mentioned above. Those "liberal and conservative" divisions setup the conditions such that something like enacting three major civil rights laws in a relatively short period of time could become the catalyst for the fracturing of our electorate.

Those 9 millions voters, who voted for Wallace and most likely some portion of those that voted for the Nixon, separated from the Democratic Party and, *in essence*, never returned to vote for a Democratic candidate

22

for president. The reason that I am confident that those Wallace and other voters never voted for the Democratic candidate after 1968 (excluding 1976 of course) was that the popular voter never increased significantly above the linear trend line from 1972 to 2000. There would have been an increase in the popular vote beyond the trend line for the Democratic candidate if the Wallace voters or any other group of Non-Democratic voters voted.

One last thought. The original issues that existed in the 60's were not necessary the issues that kept the electorates split for thirty years. The new "wedge" issues of the 70's, 80's and 90's such as abortion, gun control, and gay rights, all became supplemental or replacement issues that kept the two electorates separated.

Were There Other Associated Trends?

If the electorate had been fractured with the end result being "the Democratic Trend" on one side, what might have occurred on the other side? Could there have been a trend on the Non-Democratic side?

The initial premise was that the electorate had been fractured and the Non-Democratic portion could be categorized into two distinct types of voters (Republican and Non-Major Party).

My hypothesis was that if there truly was a fracturing of our electorate that left only two types of candidates existing on one side, then, there should be a voting pattern that reflects voting for only two catgories of candidates. In other words, the pattern should reflect two types of candidates or Parties directly taking voters away from the other. This would not be the case if three candidates or Parties were battling for the same voters. In a scenario with three candidates they each can take votes away from each other, not just from one single candidate.

To illustrate, Figure 1-11 depicts a simple two Party race. The graph clearly shows a unique pattern. The pattern is a "mirroring" of the two Party's votes. The reason why the mirror image existed was due to the Party's candidates vying for the same voters. In the example, if 100 voters turned out and one Party received 86 votes then the other Party must have received 14 votes. If one Party received 90 votes then the other Party must have received 10 votes. Essentially, one Party receives a certain amount of votes while the other receives the remaining amount. This example assumed 100 total voters for each election. The result if plotted on a graph is a mirroring of one Party with the other. It is important to note that the example could have reflected several Non-Majority parties, combined into one total vote amount instead of a single candidate or Party.

Therefore, I thought that if I could find a pattern similar to the one shown in Figure 1-11, then that would be additional evidence of the fracturing of our electorate. As a result, I plotted the votes cast for the Republican and sum of all Other or Non-Majority candidates on a chart. The result is depicted in Figure 1-12. The 1976 election was excluded since it was an outlier.

Example of Votes Cast for Two Candidate Races

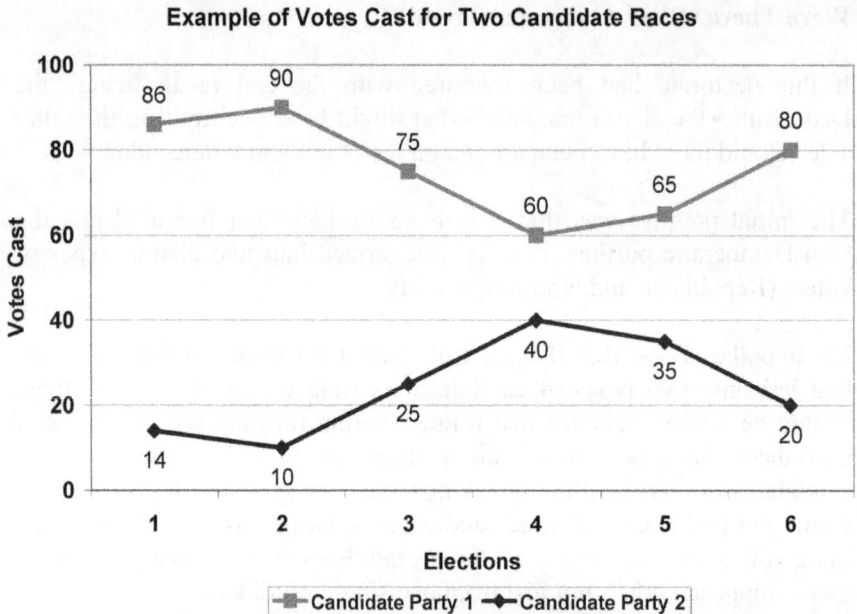

Figure 1-11 - Example of Votes Cast for Two Party Races

The results were not perfect, however, what appeared on the graph was quiet interesting. The Republican and Non-Majority candidates' popular voter reflected a mirroring of each other. You would expect a mirroring effect of Democratic and Republican candidates since our electorate essentially has a two party system. However, what was shown on the graph in Figure 1-12 was the mirroring of Republican and Non-Major Party candidates. More importantly, the votes cast for the Democratic candidates displayed a linear trend while the mirror effect occurs with Republican and Non-Major Party candidates.

Be that as it may, as you can see the result was not two perfectly symmetrical images, however they certainly gave the impression of a mirroring of two types of voters. However, the differences were enough for me to contemplate why there was not a more perfect mirror image. It then occurred to me that I had forgotten one of the options for the voters in the Non-Democrat electorate. Unlike those in the Democrat electorate some of the voters in the Non-Democrat electorate choose not to vote. There were actually three options in the Non-Democrat electorate: 1) vote for the Republican candidate; 2) vote for one of the Other or Non-Majority Party candidate; or 3) not vote at all.

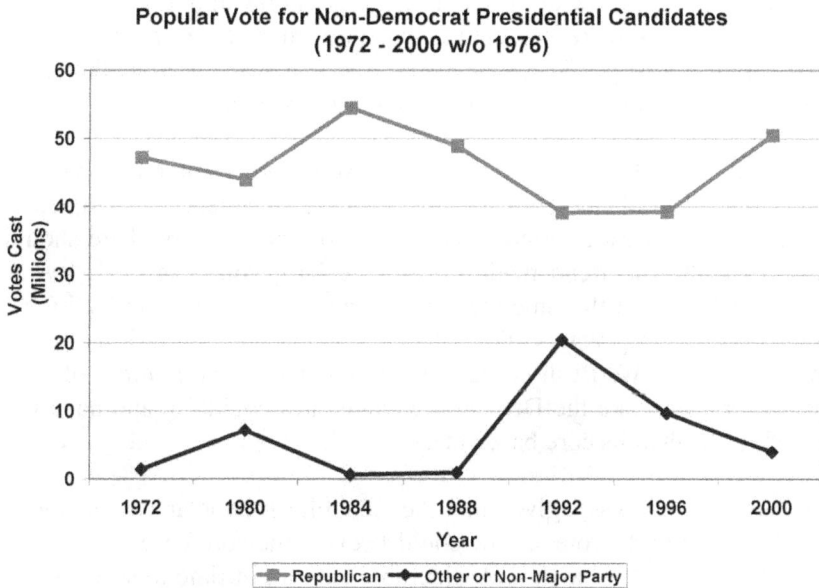

Source: Dave Leip's Atlas of U.S. Presidential Elections, uselectionatlas.org

Figure 1-12 - Popular Vote for Non-Democrat Presidential Candidates (1972-2000 w/o 1976)

The third option was the reason why the image of the votes for the Republican candidate and the combined votes for the Non-Majority Party candidate did not perfectly mirror each other. Most likely there was always a portion of the voters that did not vote and these voters did not show up on the chart.

As a matter of fact, I realized that the point of the graph that did not produce a mirror effect as much as the other elections was in 1992. It seemed that during that year, the principal Non-Majority Party candidate, Ross Perot, motivated many voters who normally do not vote, to turnout and vote for him. However, it was the results of the Republican candidate, George H. W. Bush, in the election of 1992 and 1996 that led me to contemplate another associated feature of the Phenomenon. Considering the additional voters that "turned out" to vote for Ross Perot and given the "mirror effect," the votes for George H. W. Bush should have decreased much more than it did. It was as if the popular vote for him collided with some type of "floor" that did not allow him to go any lower. I pondered, "was there something that prevented the Republican vote from dipping lower?" The conclusion was that there was another core group of voters - the "Republican" core base of voters.

Intuitively, it makes sense that if there were core Democratic base of voters, there should be core Republican base of voters. Consequently, just as the Democratic Trend consisted of core base voters, there should exist a Republican trend made up of core base voters as well. It was simply that most of the time the Republican popular vote had additional Non-Majority Party voters adding to the popular vote to mask the trend. Thus, George H.W. Bush could not dip lower than the number of core base voters. Just like the Democratic candidates could not and have not dipped lower than its core base voters.

Another question was, "given that the Republican popular vote included Non-Majority Party voters, how could I reveal the core base Republican trend?" This question took a considerable amount of time to solve. First, it was determined that since the 1992 election had so many Non-Majority Party voters "not" voting for the Republican candidate, it left only the Republican core base. Second, if I could find at least three elections that had a sizeable amount of Non-Majority Party candidates receiving a substantial amount of votes, it may reveal the Republican core base trend. My central assumption was that if the Democratic core base popular vote aligns itself along a straight line, because of population growth, so should the Republican core base voters. Consequently, I needed to find at least three elections whereby the Republican popular vote was arranged in a straight line. Two elections would produce a line, but, I needed three to display a trend. Since the 1992 election had already been discovered, I only needed to find two others.

Quickly it was realized that another election was the year that the electorate was fractured, 1968. Remember, George Wallace received a substantial amount of votes as a Non-Majority Party candidate. This should qualify as an election that should reveal the Republican core base trend.

The third election was a little more difficult to find. I reviewed the votes cast for Non-Majority Party candidates and found the election of 1948.

Popular Vote for Republican Presidential Candidates (1948, 1968 & 1992)

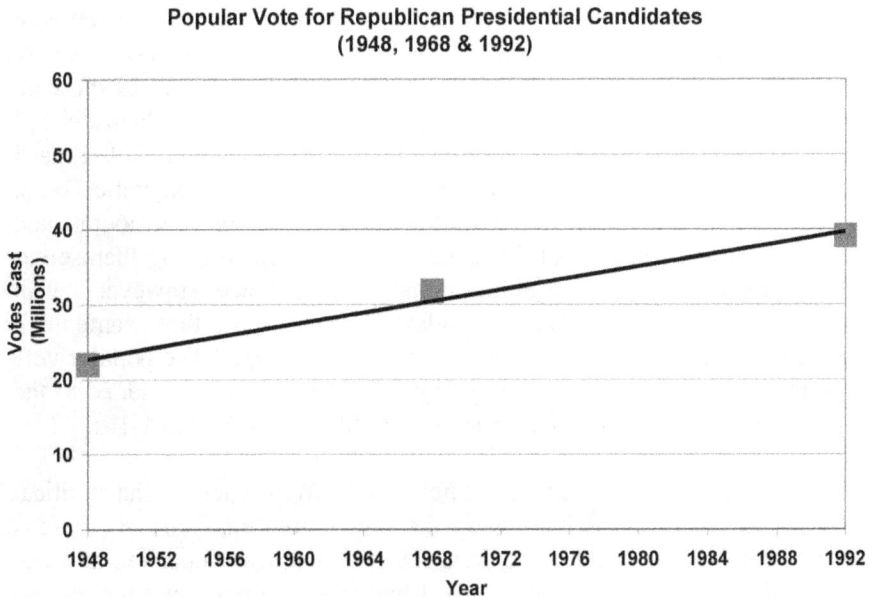

Source: Dave Leip's Atlas of U.S. Presidential Elections, uselectionatlas.org

Figure 1-13 - Popular Vote for Republican Presidential Candidates (1948, 1968, 1992)

In 1948, Governor James "Strom" Thurman ran for president under a new 3rd Party called the States Right or "Dixiecrat" Party. Yes, this was same Strom Thurman that ended up being the long serving Senator from South Carolina. Also, the Dixiecrats consisted mostly of individuals who splintered off from the Democratic Party because of the support that the Party had for several controversial civil rights planks. If this sounds familiar to you, I thought the same thing. It seemed to be a repeat of the 1968 election. However, it was prior to 1968 so it was not a repeat, it was actually foreshadowing.

I now had the three elections to prove my hypothesis. The best way to view the results was to use points on a graph. Therefore, the popular vote for the Republican candidates for the elections years of 1948, 1968, and 1992 were plotted. The results can be seen in Figure 1-13.

The votes cast remarkably seemed to align themselves in a near straight line. If you are interested in how straight or "linear" the Republican core base line is, be sure to review Chapter 6. Refer to Figure 1-7 to verify how those three elections align themselves while the other ones show no pattern. Once it was determined that these elections aligned themselves, I wondered if this was simply a unique coincidence. I then recalled that I already had proof of another core base line. It was the Democratic Trend. This would give me two baselines to plot. If the Democrat and Republican candidates had the same three elections aligning themselves in a straight line, it would be more than a coincidence. However, "what about the Non-Majority Party candidates?" What would those same three election show if I also plotted them on the same graph? The popular vote for the Democratic and Non-Majority Party candidates was added to the graph. Again, the groups were remarkably linear (see Figure 1-14).

These trends were named "baseline" trends. With each of the political groups aligning themselves using the same three elections, the results were more than a mere coincidence. Something was occurring at those three elections. Given these results, I had to develop another theory and explain this unique anomaly. One of the starting points for me was to review any unusual circumstance surrounding the three elections.

Considering these three elections, a common pattern was observed. In each of these elections there was a substantial Non-Major Party candidate. That Non-Major Party candidate garnered votes from a disgruntled population for some particular volatile issue. The issues are polarizing enough that voters diverge to their respective Party affiliation. However, the essential ingredient that forced the core base voters to reveal themselves was the Non-Major Party candidate. The Non-Major Party candidate in each of the three elections attracted the remaining voters, who were not core base voters, away from the other Major Parties.

**Popular Vote for Presidential Candidates
(1948, 1968 & 1992)**

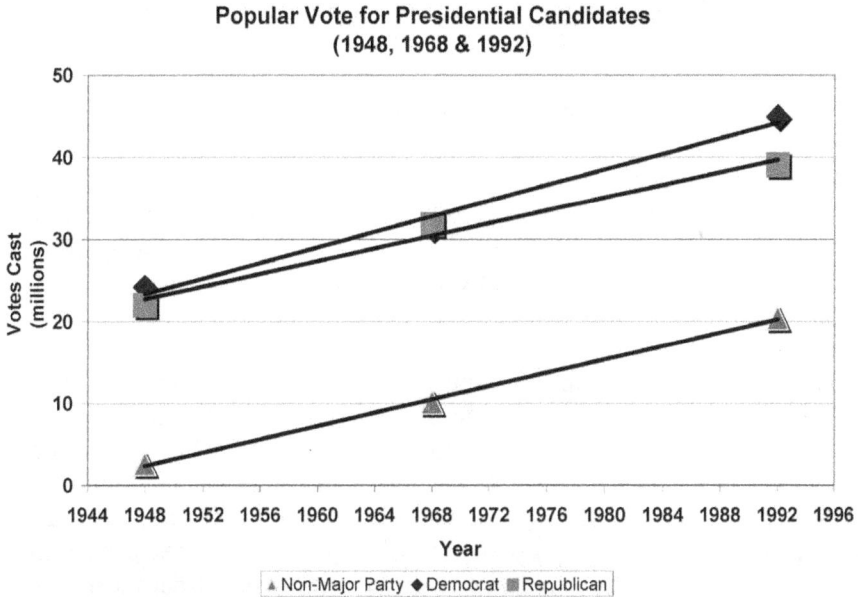

Source: Dave Leip's Atlas of U.S. Presidential Elections, uselectionatlas.org

Figure 1-14 - Popular Vote for Presidential Candidates
(1948, 1968, 1992)

To illustrate this scenario, consider the three elections. First, in 1948 the Democratic President Harry S. Truman issued two executive orders that were very controversial for its time. The two bold orders were: banning segregation in the armed forces; and guaranteeing of fair employment practices in civil service. These initiatives made President Truman the first president to address civil rights issues for African Americans since Abraham Lincoln. Although, the military took two years to implement the law, his initiatives did not sit well with some individuals, including some Democrats. The Democrats in the South were especially angered by these initiatives.

Some southern Democrats were so outraged by Truman's executive orders that it became one of the central impetuses for a group of delegates during the 1948 Democratic National Convention splintering off and forming the States Rights or "Dixiecrat" Party. The Party nominated a young Governor named James "Strom" Thurman. That year in 1948, Governor Thurman received 2.4% of the popular vote. Although Thurman received what was perceived as a relatively small amount, I concluded that this might have caused the first fissure in the electorate that was to crack in 1968 (see Chapter 2).

Next, in 1968 the Democratic President was Lyndon Johnson and the disgruntled Democratic Governor from Alabama was George Wallace. Like Strom Thurman, George Wallace ran for president under a new 3rd Party. The new third Party, called the American Independent Party, was opposed to the series of Civil Rights laws that had previously passed. Touting "States Rights" and select "blue collar" issues George Wallace received over 9.9 million votes or 13.5% of the popular vote.

The third and final anchor point, 1992, featured a different Majority candidate Party, Non-Major Party, and different issue. Yet the theme was essentially the same. This election included a Republican President, George H.W. Bush. The Non-Major Party candidate running was billionaire Henry "Ross" Perot. This election did not include a disgruntled Democrat opposed to Civil Rights. It included a disgruntle billionaire, Ross Perot, opposed to the soaring national debt and annual deficit. In fact, at one point Perot, purchased television airtime to discuss the national debt and deficit in the form of an infomercial. He received 19.7 million votes or 18.9% of the popular vote.

Because of the similar circumstance placed on these elections they can be used as points to measure the population of the core base voters of each Majority Party as well as the remaining voters who were included in Non-Majority Parties (see Chapters 9 and 13). Excited about discovering two major trends (Democratic Trend and Baseline Trend) the analysis turned toward solving the exception to the rule, the election of 1976.

What Occurred In 1976?

This question was probably the easiest to solve. First, the 1976 election was viewed as an anomaly. Therefore, some unique event, instance, or occurrence needed to be found to make it and exception. What occurred around or prior to the 1976 election that was exceptional?

In the 1976 election, the sitting President was Republican Gerald Ford and his Democratic opposition was Georgia Governor Jimmy Carter. Carter being a southern governor boded well for him in the election that year. In fact, in 1976 he carried every Southern state except for Virginia. However, one additional element contributed to the performance of Jimmy Carter that year, "Watergate."

As you are probably aware, Watergate was the name of a scandal involving Republican President Richard M. Nixon. The scandal began with five men being arrested after breaking and entering into the headquarters of the Democratic National Committee (DNC) at the Watergate hotel complex in Washington, D.C. and ended with a cover-up of the break-in. President Nixon's and his staff's problem was not the break-in itself, but that they conspired to cover-up the activities of the break-in.

Because of the scandal, congress initiated the process for the impeachment of Nixon. Ultimately, President Nixon resigned before the impeachment process could be completed. Nonetheless, Richard Nixon's resignation was the first and only resignation of a president in United States history. Gerald Ford, who was Nixon's Vice President, assumed the presidency in August of 1976. He was, in my estimation, linked to Nixon and thus to Watergate. Consequently, Watergate, an unusual and dramatic milestone for the presidency caused what I believe was the anomaly or the "exception to the rule" for the Democratic Trend. In effect, those voters that fractured off from the Democratic Party in 1968 and 1972 decided to come back for one election and vote for Jimmy Carter.

Satisfied with the answer pertaining to the anomaly of 1976, the trend line was extended four additional years to answer the question, "How did 2004 align with the Trend?"

How Did 2004 Election Align With The Trend?

By the summer of 2004, all of my major questions were answered. However, there was a question that could not be answered until November 2004. That question of course was "How did the popular vote for Democratic candidate in 2004 align with the Trend?" Therefore, after the election, the results were obtained plotted.

When the 2004 election was added to the existing trend it seemed to indicate that the popular voter for the Democratic candidate, who was Senator John Kerry, was slightly greater than the predicted trend line. A trend line has been added to the bar graph in Figure 1-15 to show the increase. Notice that the election of 2004 appears higher than the trend line, while most of the other elections do not or barely cross it. I wondered, "Why did John Kerry seem to perform better than the other Democratic candidates since 1972?"

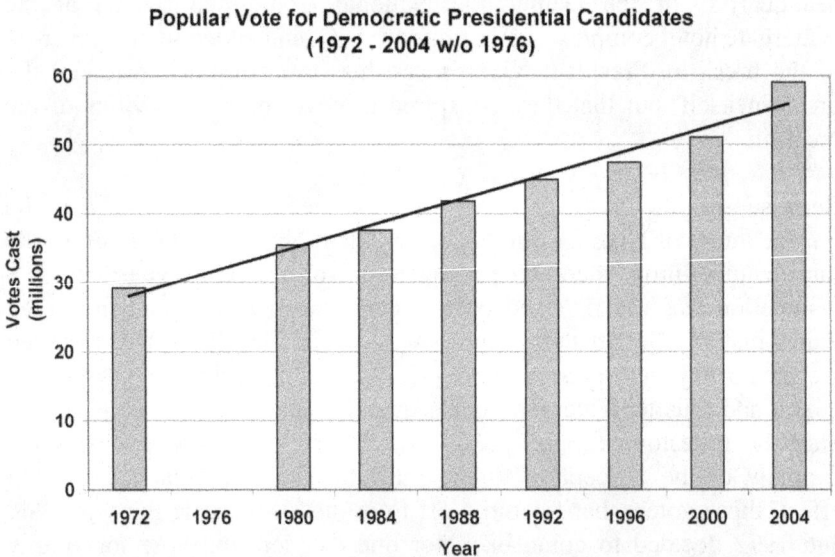

Popular Vote for Democratic Presidential Candidates
(1972 - 2004 w/o 1976)

Source: Dave Leip's Atlas of U.S. Presidential Elections, uselectionatlas.org

Figure 1-15 - Popular Vote for Democratic Presidential Candidates
(1972 - 2004 w/o 1976)

After over thirty years of the popular vote for the Democratic candidate closely following the Trend, why did the votes cast all of a sudden break away and perform better than the projected. Once again, all of the major issues and occurrences that surrounded the 2004 election had to be recalled. Unfortunately, no exceptional "direct" linkage was found. Nonetheless, three theoretical reasons why the Democratic candidate performed much better than predicted are offered below.

My first thought was that there might have been an extraordinary increase in population from 2000 to 2004. In fact, according to the U.S. Census Bureau there was an increase in the voting age population of over 13 million persons from 2000 to 2004. However, from 1984 through 2000 the largest increase from election to election was 8.9 million. This dramatic increase from the prior years led me to believe that the increase in Kerry's vote was tied to the increase in voting age population from 2000 to 2004.

Nonetheless, from 1968 to 1984 the largest increase from election to election was over 19 million. At the same time there was not any major fluctuation of the vote for the Democratic candidate since 1968 excluding 2004 and of course 1976. Although I felt that the dramatic increase in the recent voting age population from 2000 to 2004 had something to do with the increase in Kerry's vote, it would be insignificant unless a sizable percentage registered and voted for John Kerry.

Similar to the first reason the second factor centered on the reality that organizations throughout the country had registered substantial amounts of voters in preparation for the November 2004 election. In fact, the increase in registered voters from 2000 to 2004 was the largest increase from presidential election to presidential election year in thirty years. To be specific, there were over 12 million new registered voters added from 2000 to 2004. The previous two presidential election cycles (1992 to 1996 and 1996 to 2000) added 1.1 million and 1.8 million respectively (see Chapter 12). Clearly, the 2000 to 2004 cycle was substantially larger than other increases in recent years. However, these newly registered voters could not add to Kerry's votes unless they actually voted.

In 2004, exit polls from CNN revealed that 11% of the voters were first time voters. In 1996 and 2000 exit polls by CNN revealed that only 9%

of the voters were first time voter. My conclusion was that the dramatic increase in new registered voters most likely influenced the number of first time voters (although they are not necessarily the same).

This increase of 2% of first time voters (11% minus 9%) resulted in an additional 2.4 million new voters. The same exit polls indicated that Kerry received 53% of these voters. This equated to an additional 1.3 million voters than if the percentage of first time voters equated to 9% (the 1996 or 2000 levels). The additional of 1.3 million voters for Kerry did not completely answer the increase of the Trend. There must have been another factor involved.

% of Votes Cast Who Were First Time Voters
1996, 2000, 2004

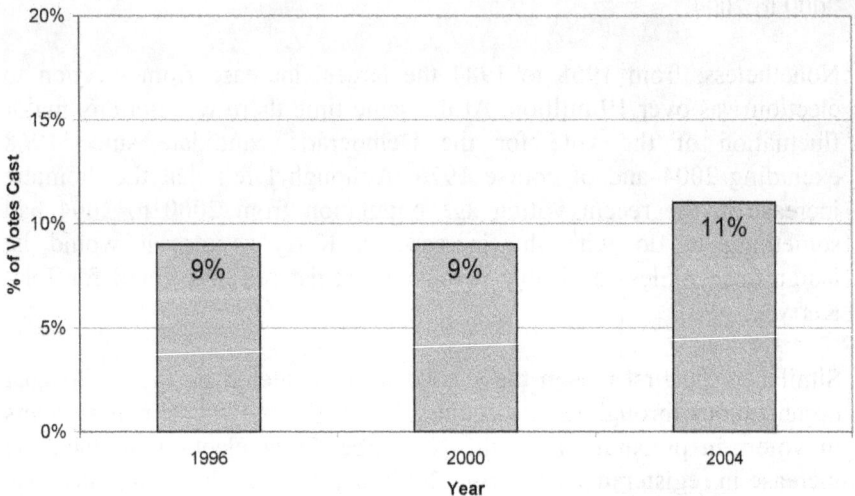

Source: CNN.com Exit Polls 1996, 2000, 2004

Figure 1-16 - % of Votes Cast Who Were First Time Voters

With additional investigation the third factor was found that contributed to the bending of the Trend. As with 1976, an issue may have arisen that changed or altered the voting electorate. The evidence was that this unknown issue did not change the electorate as much as Watergate, but it may have altered it nonetheless. There was only one issue in 2004 that was dominant, the Iraq war. Although many polls suggested a growing disagreement with the Iraq war, it could not be quantified to explain the additional votes cast for John Kerry. [22]

All and all, I felt that the jury was still out on whether the portion of voters who switched, or even those that were newly registered Democratic voters, will vote the same way as core base voters. They may simply be part of the Non-Democrat electorate or even voters who choose to not vote in the past.

On the other hand, the 2004 election could be the beginning of another electoral realignment. In other words, it may be an end to the 1968 realignment. Some say that Johnson's statement of "I think we have just delivered the South to the Republican Party for a long time to come" actually may have been "I think that we have lost the South for a Generation." If so, this may be the final reason for the deviation of 2004. The generation who removed themselves from the Democratic Party in 1968 may be passing away and being replaced by a new generation who are not as adamantly Non-Democrat. In essence our divergent electorates may be finally merging back together.

Is The Trend A Phenomenon Or Phenomena?

One of the final aspects of the Trend occurred to me while I was at home glancing at my computer that displayed a nationwide map. At the time I was sitting in my chair contemplating various aspects to the Democratic Trend Phenomenon. Suddenly, the map allowed me to visualize the Democrat Electorate, not as a single piece, but as collection of small interconnecting pieces. In other words, since the Democratic Trend was the total popular vote of the Democratic candidate for the entire country, it in fact consisted of a collection of states added together. Consequently, I pondered that maybe the Trend obeyed the laws of geometry…"the whole is equal to the sum of its parts." In essence, maybe it was actually made up of small Democratic Trends at the state level.

---

[22] In March of 2003, a Gallup poll reveal that 75% of Americans felt the U.S. did "not" make a mistake in sending troops to Iraq. By 2004, a Gallup poll showed a fairly dramatic decrease to 48%. Consequently, it was deduced that the dramatic growing opposition to the war might have influenced a portion of the Non-Democrat electorate to switch over and vote for Kerry.

My first step in proving this hypothesis was to gather the popular vote at the state level for the presidential elections from 1972 to 2004 (excluding 1976). I then began running analysis to verify if any states had "linear" popular votes. What I found was that there were 26 states that were considered to closely follow the pattern[23] of the Democratic Trend. Review Chapter 10, to view which particular states displayed the effects of the Trend.

After reviewing the state level trends I concluded the following. First, residing in each state were the Democratic voters that made up the Democratic Trend. Second, at the national level these voters were summed together to form the popular vote for the Democratic candidate for president. Third, at the state level some of these voters would and did move from state to state. Forth, this movement from state to state degraded the consistency of the Trend, at the state level, and the linear aspect of the Trend. Even though, many states population remained consistent enough to reflect the Democratic Trend.

Content with the results, I then looked at the state level using baseline trends. What was discovered was that each of the baseline trends (Democrat, Republican, and Other or Non-Major Party) reflected throughout the majority of states.

The result of the state analysis directed me back to the statements of President Johnson. His concerns of losing the South turned out to be accurate. Nonetheless, I do not think that even President Johnson could have foreseen that the fracturing of our electorate would have occurred not only in the South, but in a majority, if not all, of the states. And thus, the Democratic Trend was determined to not just be a phenomenon, but instead a phenomena.

What Does the Future Hold for the Democratic Trend?

If the Democratic Trend continues to exist it should be possible to predict the 2008 election and potentially other future elections. Therefore, the Trend was used to determine the estimated popular vote that Democratic candidates, Senator Barack Obama, would receive in November 2008.

---

[23] Using regression analysis 26 states had greater than a .85 Coefficient of Determination.

Once again, a formula was developed using linear regression for the Democratic Trend (see Chapter 13). The estimated popular vote obtained by Barack Obama for the November 2008 election was calculated to be an unimpressive 59.4 million. This estimate seemed rather low. In fact, John Kerry received 59 million votes in 2004, an amount roughly 5 million more than the Trend projected (54 million).

Given the results in 2004, the Democrat Electorate may be suddenly trending at a higher rate than the 1972 to 2000 pace. Thus, these additional 5 million voters were added to the estimate of core Democratic base voters.[24] Consequently, in 2008 if Barack Obama obtains a popular vote close to or greater than 64 million, it can be assumed that the Democrat Electorate has expanded and the Trend has been altered. It is important to note that if an increase, similar to the one in 2004, occurs in 2008, Senator Obama could potentially receive 69 million votes or even more.

Nevertheless, because of the existence of the Democratic Trend, a much more interesting projection was made when determining the "percentage" of the popular vote for the 2008 election (see Chapter 13). Trend formulas were developed using the percentage of the popular vote of the Democratic and Non-Democratic candidates (from 1972 to 2004). Using the derived formulas, the projected percentage of the votes cast for 2008 for the Non-Democratic candidate was calculated to be *48.9%*. Considering the accuracy of the trend lines, which was determined to be better than 94.7%, Senator John McCain *plus the other Non-Majority Party candidates combined* were predicted to obtain somewhere between 46.4% to as much as 51.4% of the vote in 2008. On the other hand, the Democratic candidate's estimate turned out to be *51.1%*. Once again taking in account of the range in accuracy, Senator Barack Obama was projected to garner between 48.4% to 53.8% of the popular vote in 2008. If a reasonable estimate of at least 2% was anticipated for the Non-Majority Party candidates combined, Senator John McCain would be projected to receive 46.9%, with Senator Barack Obama receiving 51.1% (with an error for McCain as much as $\pm$ 2.5% and Obama as much as $\pm$ 2.7%). Given the margin of 4.2%, Barack Obama stands an excellent

---

[24] By 2008 the additional voters could expand to greater than 5 million.

chance of becoming the winner of the popular vote. That is if you exclude the "Bradley Effect."[25]

Not only that, the Democratic candidates were projected to receive 52.6%, 54.1%, and 55.6% of the popular vote over the next three elections (2012, 2016, and 2020). If accurate, the Democratic candidate for president would be destined to continue to win the popular vote unless another major *realignment* of the electorate takes place.

Even so, one of the most ironic aspects of this theory was the realization that in 2008 there is great opportunity for Democratic candidate, Barack Obama, to acquire a substantial amount of votes from the Non-Democrat electorate. Although it may be that in 2004, John Kerry may have been the first recipient to garner votes from the Non-Democrat electorate, Barack Obama may be the first Democratic candidate to accomplish this goal in a major way. [26] With his propensity to seemingly attract Independent or even Republican voters[27], along with the possibility that the electoral fracturing may be ending, he just may be successful. Consequently, Barack Obama's success would be ironic due to the remarkable reality that the Democratic candidate who was the first to appeal to a sizeable amount of Non-Democratic voters would be an African American. Some of those Non-Democratic voters or at least their preceding family members had initially shifted away from voting for the Democratic candidates because of their opposition to civil rights laws. On the other hand, the 2008 election may result in the Democratic candidate's popular vote moving back to the same trend line that existed for thirty years. However, if I were forced to choose, I would predict that, *"change is coming to America."*

---

[25] A term named after Los Angeles Mayor Thomas "Tom" Bradley to denote a decrease in the actual vote total compared to the poll results for an African American or Non-White candidate. It is also known as the Wilder Effect.

[26] Of course, excluding Jimmy Carter and the election of 1976.

[27] Richard Wollfe, *When Republicans Endorse Obama*, February 1, 2008, Newsweek.com.

Chapter 2

Prelude to a Trend

*"All progress is precarious, and the solution of one problem
brings us face to face with another problem."*

Dr. Martin Luther King, Jr.

Introduction

In the previous chapter, the mystery of the Democratic Trend was
unraveled. The root cause should now be reviewed in further detail. This
chapter discusses the central basis of this predictable Trend and how one
solution can sometimes create another problem, or as Dr. Martin Luther
King, Jr. stated, *"All progress is precarious, and the solution of one
problem brings us face to face with another problem."*

The First Crack in the Electorate

We should first review the circumstances that existed to precipitate the
formation of the Trend. Thus, we begin with an election that occurred
sixty years ago. The year was 1948. The President was Harry S. Truman.
The upcoming election that year would prove to be foreshadowing for
another election that would come twenty years later. In 1948, President
Truman issued two executive orders that were very controversial for that
time. The two bold executive orders were: banning segregation in the
armed forces; and the guaranteeing of fair employment practices in the
civil service. These initiatives made President Truman the first president
to address civil rights issues for African Americans since Abraham
Lincoln. Although the military took two years to implement the law, his
initiatives did not sit well with some Democrats, especially ones in the
south.

As a side note, another foreshadowing event occurred in 1948 when an
organization known as the Americans for Democratic Action (A.D.A.)
drafted a minority report. The report included an amendment
commended Truman for "his courageous stand on the issue of civil

rights." A.D.A.'s spokesman at that time was Hubert Horatio Humphrey Jr., the mayor of Minneapolis, Minnesota. Hubert Humphrey will end up playing a central role in the next phase of the creation of the Trend twenty years later.

Running in the upcoming presidential election of 1948 against Truman was the Republican Thomas E. Dewey. Also running in the 1948 election was a relatively young Governor James "Strom" Thurman of South Carolina. Thurman, who was a Democrat at the time, ran for president under a new 3rd Party called the States Rights or "Dixiecrat" Party. The Dixiecrats consisted mostly of individuals who splintered off from the Democratic Party because of the support that the Party had for several controversial civil rights planks.

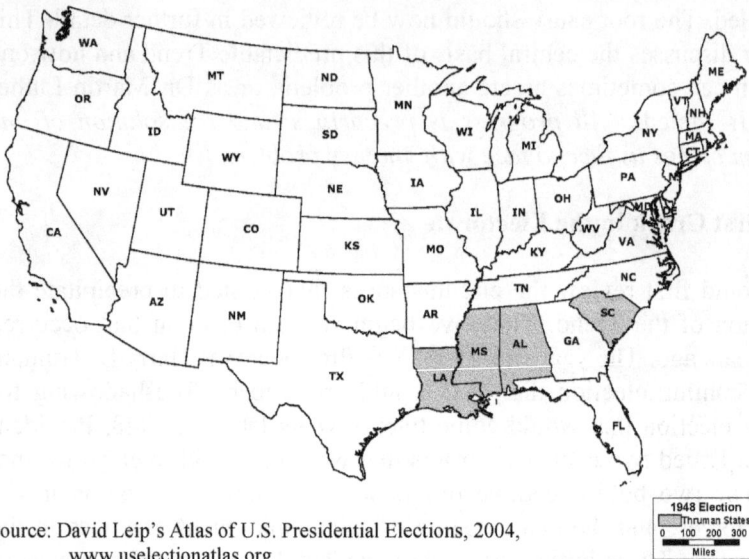

Source: David Leip's Atlas of U.S. Presidential Elections, 2004,
www.uselectionatlas.org

Figure 2-1 - States Won By Strom Thurman in the 1948 Election

During the 1948 election, Thurman received over a million votes and a little over 2 percent (2.4%) of the popular vote. Although Thurman received a relatively small percentage of the popular vote, he carried four southern states: Alabama, Louisiana, Mississippi, and of course his home state of South Carolina (see Figure 2-1). To illustrate how unusual this was, since that time there has been only one other Non-Majority candidate to win a state. Nevertheless, as a result of Thurman's failed bid for the presidency, the Dixiecrat Party quickly dissolved after the election. As a consequence, the old Dixiecrat voters would ultimately return and vote for the Democratic candidate in future elections. Nevertheless, this election produced the first "fissure" in the voting electorate.[28]

Even though Thurman's run for the presidency was unsuccessful, it foreshadowed what was yet to come in 1968[29] - that is to say, embittered Democrats and a substantial splintering off from the Democrat electorate.

The Turbulent 60's

Notwithstanding the upheaval caused by the civil rights movement, the 1960's were ripe for some type of dramatic political event. In fact, some have labeled this period "The Turbulent 60's."[30] For example, during the 1960's there were several notable assassinations, including: John F. Kennedy, Martin Luther King Jr., Robert F. Kennedy, and Malcolm X. In addition: the cold war heated up; a sexual revolution began; recreational use of drugs was thriving; and last but certainly not least the war in Vietnam was causing unrest in the country.

Each of these major occurrences of the 60's carried social, cultural, and more importantly political implications. Furthermore, the political dimensions were polarizing. That is to say that the political gap between those that considered themselves liberal (associated with the Democrats) and those who considered themselves conservative (associated with the Republicans) widen. In other words voter who made up our voting electorate were being pulled apart by the issues of the 60's. Consequently, this increase in the political distinctions in addition to the critical differences on civil rights set the stage for an extremely polarized electorate and the "mother of all electoral realignments."

---

[28] For the purpose of this book, the voting electorate includes voters who vote for the office of president.

[29] Thurman later switched his party from Democrat to Republican in 1964.

[30] Greenhaven Press's ten book series, "The Turbulent 60's" explores this remarkably decade.

The Realigning Election

The conflict during the early 60's were simply setting the stage for the election of 1968. Twenty years after Strom Thurman's bid for the presidency in 1948, the fracturing that almost occurred completed its course. Although the years had changed the central issue remained the same - civil rights. The year was 1968. The President this time was Lyndon Baines Johnson. The disgruntled ex-Democratic candidate this time was Governor George Corely Wallace of Alabama.

Like Strom Thurman, Wallace ran for president under a new 3rd Party called the American Independent Party. Also, like Thurman, Wallace *was* a Democrat. Last but not least, similar to Thurman's Party, an underlying theme of the American Independent Party was the opposition to a series of civil rights laws. Specifically, this included the 1964 Civil Rights Act, 1965 Voting Rights Act and more importantly the 1968 Civil Rights Act otherwise known as the Fair Housing Act. The importance of the 1968 Fair Housing Act was that it prohibited discrimination in the sale, rental and financing of housing. In essence the Act gave African Americans the right to purchase or rent homes located in predominantly white neighborhoods. For some whites, this was the proverbial last straw that broke the camel's back. Or, in this case the last straw that split the electorate apart.

Even though Wallace attempted to shift the focus of the American Independent Party platform to communism and blue-collar issues, civil rights or specifically "States' Rights" remained an umbrella issue during the campaign of 1968. States' Rights, at that time, simply meant that the federal government would no longer interfere with the rights of a State to enact or modify their own civil rights laws, specifically for African Americans. Of course pushing for States' Rights was done to appeal to many white voters in the southern states.

But unlike Thurman, George Wallace received over 9.9 million votes and over 13.5% of the popular vote.[31] Consequently, Wallace obtained the largest popular vote, at that time, for a 3rd Party candidate since 1924[32] (see Figure 2-2).

---

[31] U.S. Census Bureau, *Statistical Abstract of the United States*, 2001
[32] In 1924 Robert LaFollette of the Independent Progressive candidate received 17% of the popular vote.

**Popular Vote in Presidential Elections
(1964 to 1972)**

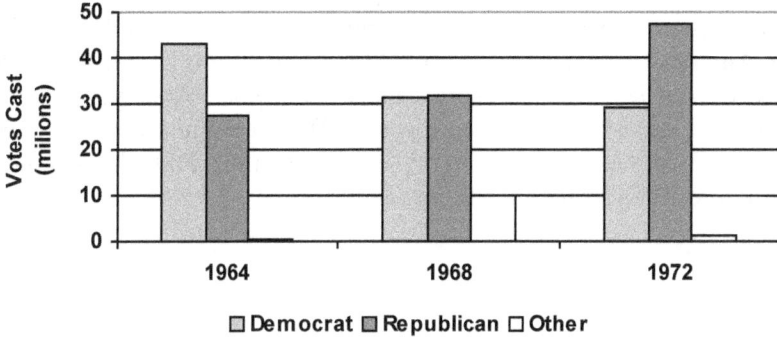

Source: U.S. Census Bureau Statistical Abstract of the U.S., 2004 (Table HS-52)

Figure 2-2 - Popular Vote in Presidential Elections
(1964 - 1972)

In order to fully understand the tenor of Wallace's campaign of 1968, we should first recall his gubernatorial election in Alabama that occurred only a few years earlier in 1962. Wallace was elected governor of Alabama on a pro-segregation, pro-States' Rights platform. In his infamous inaugural speech, he stated: "segregation now, segregation tomorrow, and segregation forever." In addition, in June of 1963, he stood in front of a schoolhouse door at the University of Alabama in an attempt to stop the desegregation of that institution by the enrollment of two African-American students.[33]

Later in 1964, using his recognized public image created by the University of Alabama controversy, Wallace ran, albeit unsuccessfully, for the Democratic nomination for president. Wallace remaining in the Democratic Party and seeking the nomination is an important factor in unraveling the origin of the Democratic Trend Phenomenon. Because Wallace ran for the nomination of Democratic Party he was essentially condoning working within the system of the Democratic Party.

---

[33] Vivian Malone and James Hood were blocked from entering the University of Alabama in 1963.

Consequently, there was no splintering of the Democrat electorate and President Lyndon Johnson, a Democrat, cruised to an easy victory (see Figure 2-2).

Nevertheless, in 1968, Wallace abandoned the Democratic Party to form the American Independent Party. Similar to Strom Thurman in 1948, Wallace carried five southern states: Alabama, Arkansas, Georgia, Louisiana, and Mississippi (see Figure 2-3). Since Wallace was no longer working within the framework of the Democratic Party his candidacy would prove devastating to the Democrats.

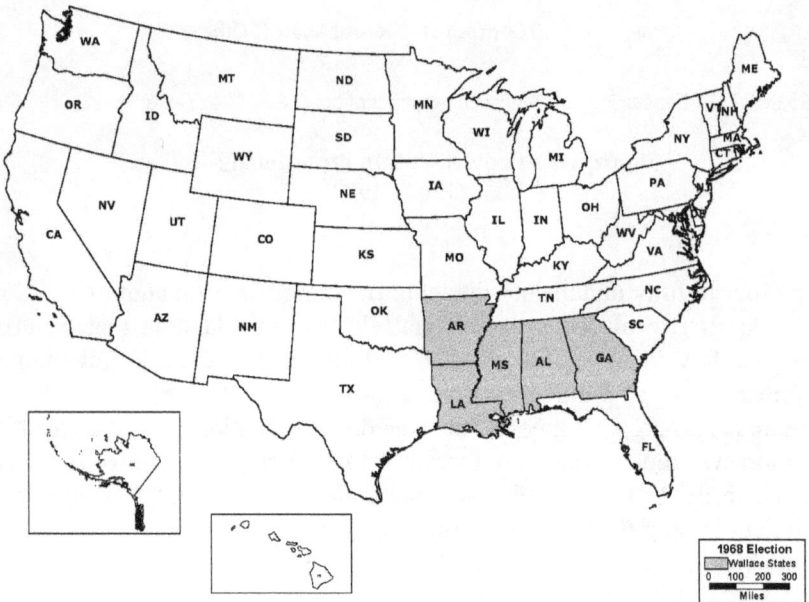

Source: David Leip's Atlas of U.S. Presidential Elections, 2004,
www.uselectionatlas.org

Figure 2-3 - States Won By Wallace in the 1968 Election

During the same time that Wallace was adamantly against the newly enacted federal Civil Rights and Voting Rights laws, Richard Milhous

Nixon, the Republican, began deploying the "Southern Strategy."[34] The Southern Strategy was aligned almost perfectly with George Wallace's position in that it promoted "States' Rights" in order to appeal to many southern white voters.

Thus, the voters had a choice - Democrats opposing States' Rights while Republicans and American Independent Partys supporting it. The southern voters did make a choice. The Republican candidate, Richard Nixon, carried three "Deep South"[35] states while Wallace carried five. The Democratic candidate, Hubert Humphrey, ultimately carried no "Deep South" states.

The popular vote for Humphrey[36], totaled over 31.3 million while the votes cast for Nixon, was only slightly higher at 31.9 million (see Table 2-1). The electoral outcome that Wallace ultimately garnered was over 9.9 million votes.

Table 2-1 - Popular Vote in Pres. Elections, 1964-1972
(millions)

	1964	1968	1972
Democrat	43.1	31.3	29.2
Republican	27.2	31.8	47.2
Other	.03	10.2	1.4

Source: U.S. Census Bureau Statistical Abstract of the United States, 2004

Since Wallace ran as a Democrat in the prior presidential election (1964) and had a base that came from the Democratic south, arguably a case can be made that his candidacy in 1968, shifted enough votes away from Humphrey to allow Nixon to win the popular vote.[37] Not only did Wallace possibly shift votes away from Humphrey in 1968, his candidacy was the catalyst for a trend that would continue for at least the next three decades. In essence, those voters that voted for Wallace in

---

[34] The Southern Strategy enabled Richard Nixon to compete and win in the Democratically dominated south.
[35] Deep South states are defined as: Alabama, Arkansas, Georgia, Florida, Mississippi and Louisiana, South Carolina, and Tennessee.
[36] Coincidentally, Hubert Humphrey was one of the central members of congress that lead the push for civil rights when Strom Thurman ran for President in 1948.
[37] See www.presidentelect.org/art_sheppard_e2000an.html

1968 did not and have not ever returned back to vote for the Democratic candidate for president - with one exception, 1976.

Chapter 3

The New Democrat Electorate

*"I think we have just delivered the South to the
Republican Party for a long time to come."*

Lyndon B. Johnson

Introduction

Because of the increasing polarization of the 1960's, stress had been
building on the electorate since 1948. Ultimately, this stress, in addition
to the support that certain Democratic leaders placed on passing civil
rights laws, was strong enough to cause a major political realignment that
resulted in the creation of a new Democrat Electorate. This political
realignment was predicted by President Johnson's legendary statement of,
*"I think we have just delivered the South to the Republican Party
for a long time to come."*[38]

Predicting Realignments or Trends in the Past

Political analysts have forecasted major realignments in the electorate for
decades. One of the pioneers in the field of political analysis was Louis
Bean. Ironically, the 1948 presidential election played a key roll in
Bean's prominence.[39] He leaped into celebrated distinction when he
predicted that in 1948 Harry Truman, the Democratic president at the
time, would beat Thomas Dewey, the Republican challenger. At that
time all other major analysts predicted a win for Dewey. One of the most
famous pictures of that era was of Truman holding up a *Chicago Daily
Tribune* newspaper with a headline that read, "Dewey Defeats Truman."
Bean of course was correct and the newspaper was wrong. For that

---

[38] New York Times, *Divisive Words: News Analysis; G.O.P.'S 40 Years Of
Juggling On Race* 2002, Adam Clymer.
[39] Also Ironic, Bean had deep concerns about the splintered "Dixiecrat" party
stripping votes away from Truman.

prognostication, in 1951, the magazine *Business Week* called him "The Best-Known Prophet Since Daniel."[40]

One of the fundamental concepts of Bean's forecasting centered on "political cycles," or as he called them "political tides." These cycles or tides were reoccurring and lasted for approximately two or three decades. Like tidal waves, the political dominance would flow in giving rise to a new party control.

However, what occurred in 1968 was not a simple political tidal wave change. It was another type of natural phenomenon, an earthquake. The stress that had been building on the voting electorate, due to the growing pressure to adopt and implement civil rights laws, had gotten to the breaking point. Like stress that is placed on tectonic plates in the earth, the pressure builds to a certain point, and then fracturing begins. In other words, an earthquake occurs. In this case the earthquake was a major fracturing or "realignment" of the voting electorate.[41] The earthquake analogy is only appropriate up to a point. After an earthquake, the plates that were shifted eventually return to rest and connect back together. In the 1968 electoral earthquake, there was a complete separation with two or more fractured pieces of the electorate never coming back together. In essence, once the total voting electorate separated, two distinct electorates were created.[42] More importantly, each of these new voting electorates contained voters who very seldom crossed over to the other electorate.

The fragmentation of some voters from the Democrat electorate is the crux of the predictable Trend. Here lies the first key to unraveling mystery of the Phenomenon. Once a sizable number of voters were removed; the Democrat electorate was left with a smaller and more consistent group of voters. In essence, the Democrat electorate had now become almost entirely the loyal base voters (see Chapter 6). Consequently, those remaining individuals were extremely reliable when it came to voting for the Democratic candidate for president. An important note is that this phenomenon only occurred at the presidential

---

[40] Business Week, August 18, 1951 pg 66.
[41] Political Scientist V.O. Key called these realignments "critical" elections.
[42] See Chapter 4 – The Non-Democrats.

level. [43] Those individuals that splintered off continued to vote for Democratic candidates at the state and local level for years to come.[44] Nonetheless, the same voters, in addition to a proportional amount of newly registered voters continue to vote for the Democratic candidate.

On the other hand, all of those voters that separated from the Democrat electorate in 1968 did not become Republicans. Most were and still are purely Non-Democrats (see Chapter 4). Here lies the second key. Non-Democrats will either not vote or vote for a Party besides Democrat.

A Predictable Trend

There was no indication of a consistent predictable Trend in the popular vote for the Democratic candidate from 1948 to 1968 (see Figure 3-1).

Democractic Candidates Popular Vote (1948 - 1972)

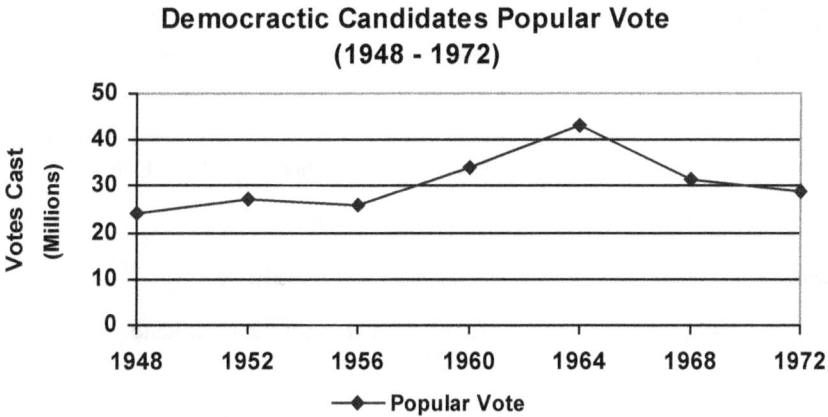

Source: Dave Leip's Atlas of U.S. Presidential Elections, uselectionatlas.org

Figure 3-1 - Popular Vote for the Democratic Candidate
(1948 - 1972)

After the election of 1968 the fragmentation of the Democrat electorate continued to erode slightly until the 1972 election. Essentially, the voting

---

[43] It is important to note that this phenomenon exists at the Presidential level and not necessarily at the state or lower levels.
[44] Democrats continue to win at U.S. Senate and House elections and lower levels until the 1990's.

electorate for the Democratic candidate for president "bottoms" out in 1972[45] (see also Figure 3-1).

From this point on, with the exception of the 1976 election, the popular vote for the Democratic candidate would always increase in a consistent fashion. In other words the votes cast would follow a predictable Trend, from election to election (see Figure 3-2).

'

**Democractic Candidate Popular Vote
(1972 - 2004)**

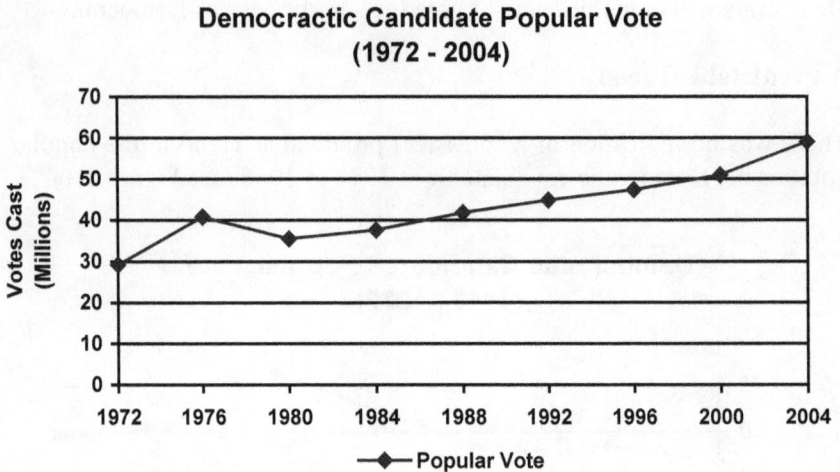

Source: Dave Leip's Atlas of U.S. Presidential Elections, uselectionatlas.org

Figure 3-2 - Popular Vote for the Democratic Candidate
(1972 -2004)

Once the assumption is made that the votes cast for the Democratic candidate consists of only steadfast reliable Democrat voters, who essentially always vote, it is easy to see how the popular vote becomes predictable. In essence, the vote for the Democratic candidate from 1972 to 2004 (excluding 1976), for the most part, does not consist of Independent or Republican voters that may vote for the Democrat. It does not consist of voters who swing back and forth between voting for Democratic candidates and candidates of other Parties. It only consists of voters that always vote for the Democratic candidate. On the other hand,

---

[45] This "bottoming out" most likely was due to the election of 1968 included some "hold-outs" of the Non-Democrats that would ultimately split off from the Democratic Party in 1972.

the Republican candidate's votes consist of core Republican voters in addition to voters who swing between Other (Non-Majority Party) candidates and simply not voting (see Figure 3-3).

It is important to stress the point that this does not mean that the Democratic candidate receives absolutely no votes from the Non-Majority Party or Republican voters. It simply means that those types of voters make up such a small portion of the popular vote for the Democratic candidate. Likewise, a very small percentage Democratic voter may vote for Republican or Other candidates.

Republican Candidate Popular Vote (1972 - 2004)

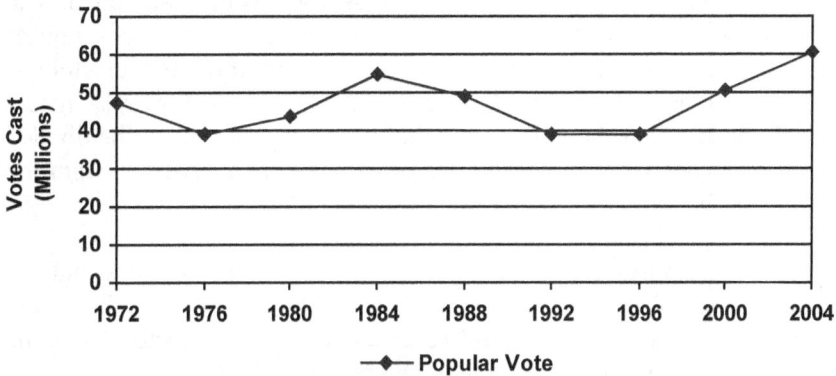

Source: Dave Leip's Atlas of U.S. Presidential Elections, uselectionatlas.org

Figure 3-3 - Popular Vote for the Republican Candidate (1972 -2004)

In addition, there are most likely voters that when asked (i.e. polled) will self-identify themselves as an Independent voter but consistently vote for the Democratic candidate for president.[46] The end result is that when these individuals vote in presidential elections they vote only for or mostly for the Democratic candidate. Thus, when polled they may

---

[46] This would result in tracking or exit polls showing a higher percentage of Independent voters voting for the Democratic candidate. A similar situation most likely occurs with Republican voters.

respond that they are independent; however, they remain part of the Democrat Electorate in presidential elections.

To demonstrate how consistent the popular vote for the Democratic candidate had become, the elections from 1988 though 2000 could have been predicted ahead of time with a 97.4% to 99.5% accuracy (see Chapter 8). The prediction for the 2004 election would have been somewhat less accurate at 91.4% (see Chapter 8). The reduction in accuracy for the 2004 election will be discussed in Chapter 12.

Sustaining the Fractured Electorate

In order for the Democratic Trend to be sustained for over thirty years, the fracturing of the voting electorate must have been maintained. The very existence of the Phenomenon relies on the continued separation of the two electorates - Democrat and Non-Democrat. If the two electorates ever merge back together, the Democratic Trend and Mirror Effect would vanish. Thus, how did the voting electorate continue to be divided? The answer lies with something that most of us are exposed to from the day we are born.

Since the pressures of enacting controversial civil rights laws and the events of the 60's seem to be the impetus for the fracturing of the voting electorate; at first glance it could be assumed that those factors continue to be the central reason. This is most likely not the case.

First, voters who were old enough to vote in 1968 may have been part of the fracturing of the electorate for certain issues. It is important to note that the same issues that existed to cause the fracturing may not be the same issues that kept or keep the two electorates apart. For example, the 60's issues such as the sexual revolution, recreational drug use, female liberation, and of course civil rights were the catalysts for the fracturing of the electorate. However, in the 70's additional "wedge" issues such as the war in Vietnam (now a Republican issue), affirmative action, and abortion became, in my estimation, seminal issues that continued the division. The 80's saw the addition of gun control and in the 90's gay rights came in to play to continue the separation between the Democrat and Non-Democrat electorate for the next couple of decades. However, as stated previously, 2004 might have been the beginning of the two electorates merging back together.

Second, what continued the separation with new registered voters was due to "Family Socialization." Family socialization is the process whereby the youth learn the rules, traditions, and acceptable interactions of a particular society. When it comes to politics, some analysts suggest that major party affiliation is passed down from generation to generation [47], Therefore, Democrats spawn Democratic children and Republican spawn Republican children.

I ultimately concluded that for over thirty years the Democrat and Non-Democrat electorates remained separate because of old and new issues that divided the electorate. Thus, the electorates have remained divided as they increased in population due mostly to "family socialization."

The Exception to the Rule - 1976?

Undoubtedly one of the fundamental questions by now is, "What happened in 1976?" The political answer is that the election of 1976 is a prime example of a "deviating election."[48] From a statistical point of view this would often be called an "outlier" or "outrider." Nonetheless, a "deviating election" is an election that, because of certain unique circumstances, does not conform to the normal political trend or cycle. Specifically, 1976 may have been an exception because of the major events that occurred a couple of years prior to the election. In particular, the 1976 election may not conform to the Trend because of the extraordinary resignation of President Richard Nixon in 1974 due to the "Watergate" scandal. In other words, those individuals who did not vote for the Democratic candidate in 1968 and 1972 may have switched back for one election cycle to vote for Jimmy Carter. One last consideration, with many of the fragmented Non-Democratic voters residing in the south[49], Carter's southern roots may have further contributed to this anomaly.

---

[47] Angus Campbell, Warren E Miller, Philip E Converse, and Donald E Stokes, The American Voter, 1960

[48] A deviating election is an election whereby the Party out of power wins the election.

[49] See Chapter 2.

Chapter 4

The Non-Democrats

"I never vote for anyone. I always vote against."

W. C. Fields

Introduction

One of the realities of The Democratic Trend is that after the major realignment in 1968, the voting electorate, at the presidential level, was fractured into two main groups: Democrats and Non-Democrats (see Figure 4-1). The simple duality of voters was caused by the pressures applied to the electorate contributing to a sizable amount of voters splintering off (see Chapter 2). This essentially left the voting electorate divided into two main groups[50]: a Democrat Electorate; and Non-Democrat Electorate[51]. These two groups made a conscience decision to not vote for the candidates of the other group or as W.C. Fields put it *"I never vote for anyone. I always vote against."*

A New Voting Electorate

When the electorate fractured it cracked leaving only "core" base voters left in Democrat electorate. These base voters always vote for the Democratic candidate in presidential elections. Furthermore, these base voters also seem to always vote in presidential elections.[52] On the other hand, those who are part of the Non-Democrat electorate, rarely or never vote for the Democratic candidate, but instead vote for the Republican,

---

[50] Many Democrats may classify themselves as Independents but vote for the Democratic candidate most of the time. Also, a small portion of the voting electorate continues to sway between the Democrat and Non–Democrat electorates.

[51] For the purpose of this book these two electorates do not consist of voters who are eligible but do not vote.

[52] The only practical way for the Democratic Trend to be linear is for the same voters to vote in each election plus a consistent percentage of new voters.

or the Other candidates[53], or they simply do not vote at all (see Table 4-1). As Table 4-1 indicates the Democratic candidate obtains votes primarily from voters who vote solely for Democrat candidates. The Non-Democrat candidates garner votes mostly from four (4) different groups: voters who vote Republican; voters who vote for Other candidates; voters who vote for both Republican and Other candidates; and voters who sometimes do not vote.

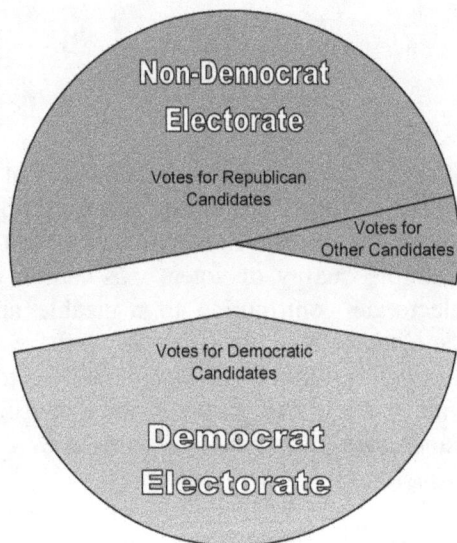

Figure 4-1 - Voting Electorate in Presidential Elections After 1968

Table 4-1 - Voting Electorate After 1968	
Democrat Electorate	**Non-Democrat Electorate**
Voters who vote for Democratic candidates	Voters who vote Republican candidates
	Voters who vote for Other candidates
	Voters who vote for Republican and Other candidates
	Voters who sometimes do not vote

The consequence of the 1968 fracturing or realignment was that the popular vote for the Democratic candidate for president became linear

---

[53] Other candidates include: Independent, Green, Reform, and other 3rd party candidates.

(i.e. in a straight line) and thus predictable. A second and just as fascinating effect was that this fracturing of the electorate caused a direct relationship between votes cast for the Republican candidate and the votes cast for the Other candidates, a second phenomenon.

A Mirror Image

Because the Non-Democrat voters vote only for the Republican or Other candidates, or they do not vote, a second phenomenon appears. Specifically, we should be able to identify some type of relationship between the popular vote for the Republican and the Other candidates. The reason for this is simple. As Table 4-1 indicates, the Non-Democrat candidates are fighting for the same voters.[54] Thus, if the Republican candidates perform well they draw voters away from the Other Candidates. Likewise, if the Other candidates perform well they draw votes from the Republican candidates. The other option is that a number of these Non-Democrats may choose to not vote. As a result, neither the Republican nor Other candidate garners these votes. It is important to note that the unstable Non-Democratic voting occurs while the Democratic candidates' popular vote increases in a consistent trend.

Since the Republican and Other candidates voters are pulling from the same pool of voters, this unique circumstance should be visible when displayed on a graph. Thus, the first step in proving a relationship between the votes cast for the Republican and Other candidates is to plot them on a scatter plot graph. Figure 4-2 displays the votes cast for the Republican and Other candidates from 1972 to 2004. What is immediately apparent is that the Republican popular vote is roughly a mirror image of the Other candidate votes.[55] Since the Republican or Other candidate voters may choose to "not vote" the graph will not form an exact mirror image.

---

[54] With the exception of a small amount of voters.
[55] The deviating election of 1976 has been removed for clarity.

Republican/Other Candidates Popular Vote
(1972 to 2004)

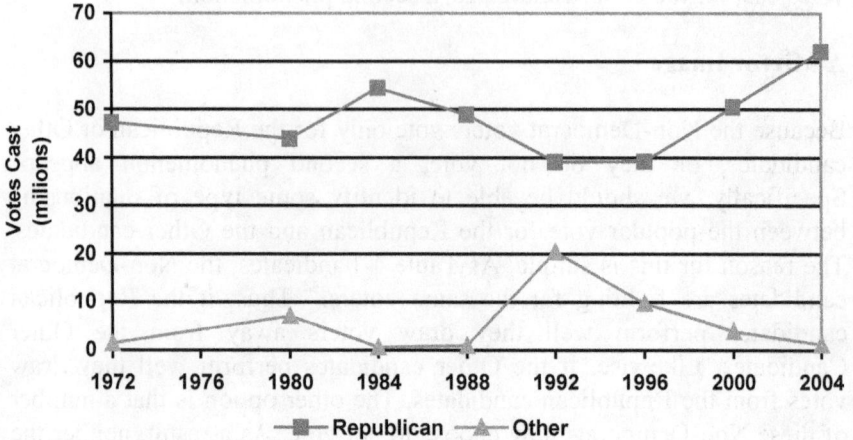

Source: Dave Leip's Atlas of U.S. Presidential Elections, uselectionatlas.org

Figure 4-2 - Republican/Other Candidates Popular Vote
(1972-2004)

Furthermore, it is important to note that the mere existence of this mirror image brings additional validation to The Democratic. The mirroring can only occur if the Republican candidates and the Other candidates are jostling for the same pool of voters. If the Democratic candidates were also fighting for the same pool of voters, in all likelihood, the graph image would *not* be mirrored.

Another method to view the relationship between the Republican and Other voters, is to view the corresponding increase or decrease from the previous election. As Table 4-2 demonstrates, a decrease in the Republican candidates votes from one year to another yield a corresponding increase for the Other candidates votes. Alternatively, when the Republican votes cast increase there is a corresponding decrease in the Other candidates votes. Thus, Table 4-2 shows the reverse interconnectivity between the Republican and Other candidates' votes cast.

Furthermore, if we modify Figure 4-1 by removing the two elections (1984 and 1992), where there were exceptional voting activity[56], the graph images become remarkably mirrored (see Figure 4-3). The unusual voting activity of 1984 and 1992[57] distorts the mirroring relationship.

Table 4-2 - Increase or Decrease from Previous Election for Republican/Other
Candidate in Presidential Elections
(1972-2004)

	72-80	80-84	84-88	88-92	92-96	96-00	00-04
Republican	Decr	Incr	Incr	Decr	Incr	Incr	Incr
Other	Incr	Decr	Decr	Incr	Decr	Decr	Decr

Note: The election of 1976 is not included.

**Rep/Other Cand Pop Vote w/o Exception Years
(1972, 1980, 1988, 1996, 2000, & 2004)**

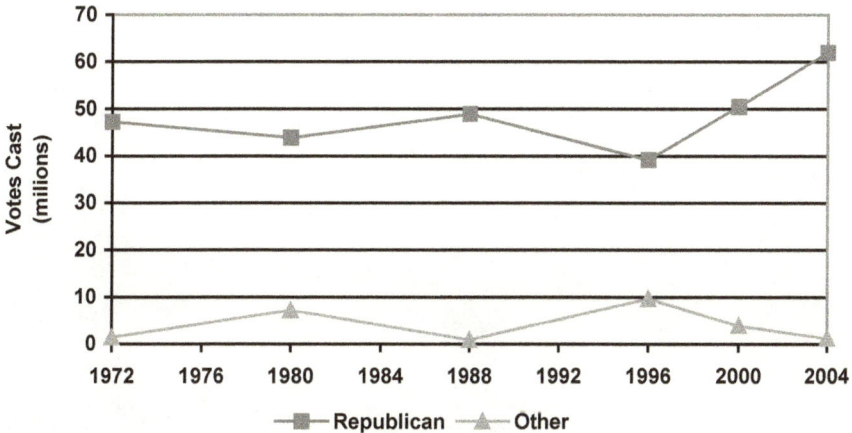

Source: Dave Leip's Atlas of U.S. Presidential Elections, uselectionatlas.org

Figure 4-3 - Rep/Other Cand Pop Vote w/o Exception Years
(1972, 1980, 1988, 1996, 2000, & 2004)

Nonetheless, the graph in Figure 4-3 exemplifies the relationship between the Republican and Other candidates' popular vote. This is to

[56] In 1984, Ronald Reagan gained an exceptionally large amount of votes, while in 1992 Ross Perot performed so well as an Independent that he brought in a substantial amount of voters that usually do not vote.
[57] See Chapter 6 – The Republican Baseline

say that when the Republican popular vote increases the Other candidates votes decreases a proportional amount. Likewise, when the Other candidates votes cast increase the Republican votes decreases. In essence, a mirror image is produced.

Chapter 5

The Reagan Non-Democrats

"Reality is frequently inaccurate."

Douglas Adams

Introduction

Much has been said and written about the Reagan Democrats. Countless reports and analyses have been developed as well as debated. In most circumstances, the Reagan Democrats have been assumed to be actual Democratic voters.[58] However, sometimes things are not the way they seem or as Douglas Adams stated *"Reality is frequently inaccurate."* Thus, does the Democratic Trend modify this common belief?

The Reagan Non-Democrats

There is no question that Ronald Reagan garnered an exceptionally large amount of votes, especially in 1984. In that year, Reagan obtained the third highest votes for President[59] in U.S. history. However, did Reagan garner votes from Democrats in 1980 and in 1984?

If the Democratic Trend is applied, the Democrat votes obtained by Reagan were not from the Democrat electorate[60] at all. They were from the Non-Democrat electorate and thus they were Non-Democrats. The reason why many analysts classify those voters as Democrats is mostly due to the 1976 election. However, as discussed in Chapter 2, the 1976 election was a "deviating" election. In essence, these Non-Democrats

---

[58] The most important aspect to the Regan Democrats was that these voters included southern Democrats in addition to northern blue–collar workers and their children.

[59] In 2004, George W. Bush obtained the highest popular vote with John F. Kerry obtained the second highest.

[60] The Democrat Electorate includes those voters that vote for the Democratic candidate for president (see Chapter 4).

came back into the fold, if you will, for one election. The reality is that most had left the Democrat electorate back in 1968. Thus, in actuality, Reagan received votes from these new Non-Democrat voters.

**Popular Vote in Presidential Elections
(1972 to 2004)**

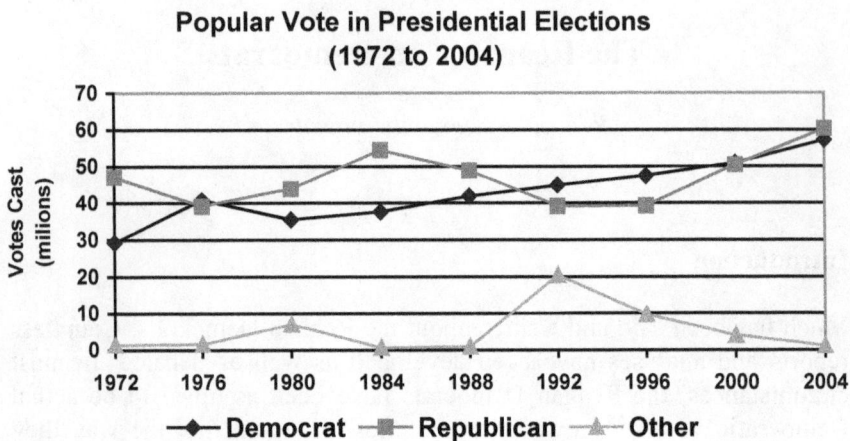

Source: Dave Leip's Atlas of U.S. Presidential Elections, uselectionatlas.org

Figure 5-1 - Popular Vote in Presidential Elections
(1972 - 2004)

Proof of Reagan not acquiring voters from the Democrat electorate lies with the Democratic Trend itself. If Reagan obtained Democratic votes, there would be an appreciable decrease in the Democratic Trend line. As Figure 5-1 shows (dark diamond shape markers), there was no appreciable decrease in the Democratic Trend in 1980 or 1984.

The standard assumption is that since Jimmy Carter, in 1980, received less votes than he did in 1976, Reagan pulled Democratic voters away from Carter. This seems reasonable unless you consider the Democratic Trend. It is true that Reagan pulled votes away from Carter, however, the election of 1976 was anomaly. The additional voters that Jimmy Carter received in 1976 were only there for a single election and did not return to vote for a Democratic candidate for president for the next three decades.

Consequently, considering the Democratic Trend, the perceived Democratic voters that voted for Ronald Reagan were not true Democratic voters (at the presidential level). They were Non-Democrats that had left the Democrat electorate, in 1968 or at least in 1972. Thus, Reagan received some votes from those who voted for Carter in 1976, but were Non-Democrats from 1968 to 1972 and from 1980 on.

Chapter 6

Other Related Trends

"We are what we repeatedly do."

Introduction

After the fracturing of 1968, in 1972, the Democrat electorate and its "core base voters" became essentially one in the same.[61] The base voters are those voters who in essence will always vote for the same Party. These voters consistently vote over and over for the same category of presidential candidate. They exemplify what Aristotle believed, which was that *"we are what we repeatedly do."*

In addition, a "baseline trend" outlines the population growth of the core base voters from election to election. Since after 1972 the Democratic Trend essentially consists of its base voters, it coincides with the Democrat baseline trend. However, "what about the Republican baseline?" and "is there a baseline trend related to the Other candidates voters?" Also, "is there a baseline trend before 1972?" This chapter discusses those questions and more.

Defining the Baseline

It turns out that the elections of 1948[62] and 1968 are not only critical elections for creating the Democratic; they also are two of three elections that define the Party's baseline voters. The third election is the election of 1992. These "baseline" elections [63] have three circumstances in common, they: 1) include major Parties which have taken significantly different positions on fundamental issues; 2) contain no clear cut winner;

---

[61] Excluding the election of 1976.

[62] 1948 votes cast excludes Alaska, Hawaii and Washington DC.

[63] These "baseline" elections are similar to the "critical" elections dubbed by a Texas political scientist named V.O. Key.

and 3) include a noteworthy third party or Non-Majority Party candidate. The combination of these circumstances polarizes the electorate such that the core or base voters gravitate to their respective major parties and the remaining voters vote for the Other or Non-Majority Party candidate(s).

Evidence that 1948, 1968, and 1992 are interrelated elections can be seen when plotted on a graph. If we plot the Democrat, Republican, and Other candidates popular vote something remarkable occurs. They each line up in a linear fashion (see Figure 6-1).

**Popular Vote in Presidential Elections
(1948, 1968 & 1992)**

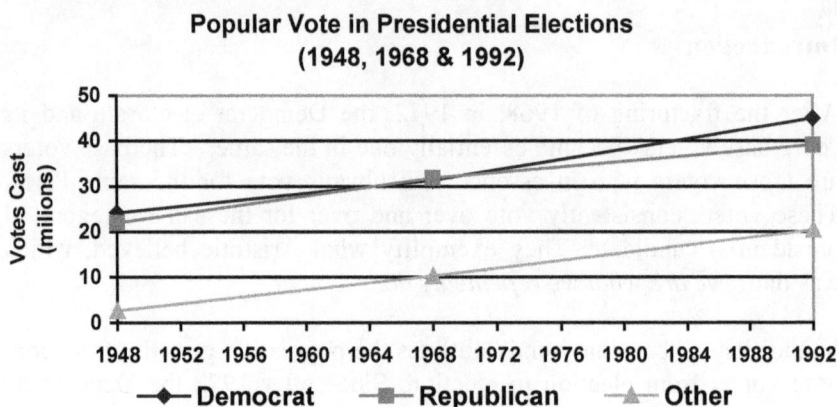

Figure 6-1 - Democrat, Republican, Other Candidates Baseline Popular Vote
(1948, 1968 & 1992)

Source: Dave Leip's Atlas of U.S. Presidential Elections, uselectionatlas.org

It is important to note that if only one of the Party's popular vote aligned itself it would be slightly interesting. However, when all three parties align themselves at the same three elections, the result is astounding. The only reasonable cause of this occurrence is that in each case the elections reveal the core base voters.

In essence, the electorate was polarized enough to draw voters to their natural base. In addition, the difference between the Party's popular vote in 1948, 1968, and 1992 is the increase in population but more specifically the increase in newly registered voters that vote.

As stated before, all of the Party's baselines are aligned along a straight line. An indication of how closely the 1948, 1968 and 1992 elections are aligned can be found by reviewing how close the popular vote matches the "best fit"[64] line that passes through all of the election points (see Chapter 9). As Chapter 9 discusses, each point on the Democrat baseline is found to be at least 95.0% accurate. The Republican and Other candidates' baselines are greater than 95.8% and 92.2%, respectively. Clearly, the accuracy shows a high degree of correlation between the elections and the Parties.

The Democrat Baseline - A Shift in 1972

Although the Democratic Trend closely aligns itself with the 1948, 1968, and 1992 elections, there was actually a minor shift in the baseline trend that occurred in 1972. Essentially, the fracturing of the electorate too an additional election cycle to completely separate. In 1968, there remained some "legacy" Democratic voters that apparently voted for Hubert Humphrey in 1968. However, by 1972 they "broke-off" and excluding 1976, would not return back to vote for the Democratic candidate for president for the next thirty years (see Figure 6-2).

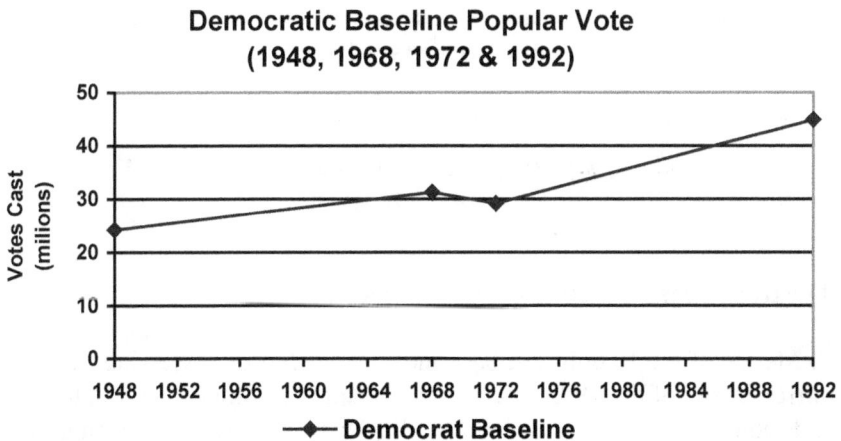

Democratic Baseline Popular Vote
(1948, 1968, 1972 & 1992)

Source: Dave Leip's Atlas of U.S. Presidential Elections, uselectionatlas.org

Figure 6-2 - Democratic Candidates Baseline Trend
(1948, 1968, 1972, and 1992)

---

[64] This is known as the regression line.

Apparently, the fracturing began in 1968 and completed in 1972 when the Democrat electorate became the core base voters. This can be seen by viewing the graph shown in Figures 6-2 and 6-3. As displayed, the actual baseline trend of the Democratic candidates' voters takes a dip from 1968 to 1972, but then continues to rise in a linear manner to 1992 and most likely beyond.

Democratic Baseline/Popular Vote (1948, 1968, 1972 & 1992)

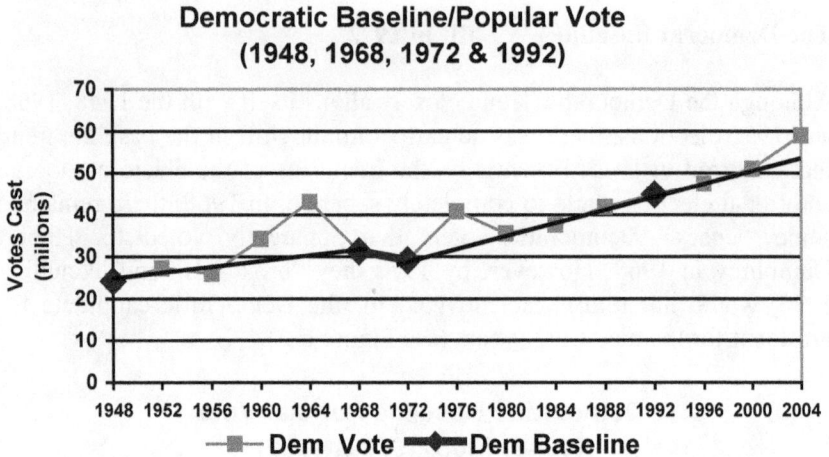

Source: Dave Leip's Atlas of U.S. Presidential Elections, uselectionatlas.org

Figure 6-3 - Democrat Candidates Baseline Trend
(1948 - 2004)

The Republican Baseline - True Validation

Existence of the Republican baseline is validated by reviewing the non-mirror image of the 1992 election. As Chapter 4 outlines, the Republican and Other candidates' popular vote displays a pattern of mirroring each other.

Thus, an increase in the Other candidates vote yields a "similar," and in most cases, proportionate decrease in the Republican votes. This is true in all elections from 1972 to 2004 except for 1992 (excluding 1976). As discussed in Chapter 4, Figure 6-4 shows that the 1992 election with Ross Perot's exceptional popular vote (included in the Other candidate's vote) did not yield a similar magnitude of decline in the Republican's votes. The reason for the disproportionate decline mostly lies with the Republican baseline.

**Republican/Other Candidates Popular Vote
(1972 to 2004)**

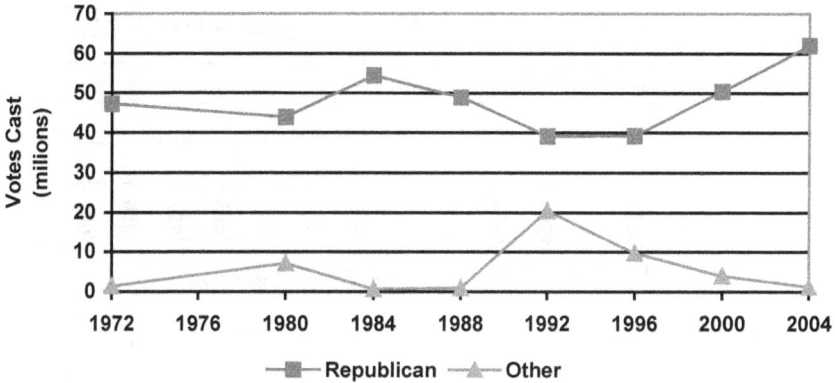

Source: Dave Leip's Atlas of U.S. Presidential Elections, uselectionatlas.org

Figure 6-4 - Republican/Other Candidates Popular Vote
(1972-2004)

As Figure 6-5 displays, the decrease in votes due to the increase in the Other candidate's votes, reached the Republican baseline. Furthermore, the Republican candidate should never receive votes less than their baseline. Therefore, Ross Perot had reached the limit of persuading voters who voted Republican. Consequently, as expected, excluding a very small dip in 1964 and 1996[65], the Republican candidate has not received fewer votes than the baseline since 1948.

---

[65] In 1964 and 1996, the Republicans, Barry Goldwater and Bob Dole, received slightly less votes than the baseline.

**Republican Baseline/Popular Vote
(1948, 1968, 1992)**

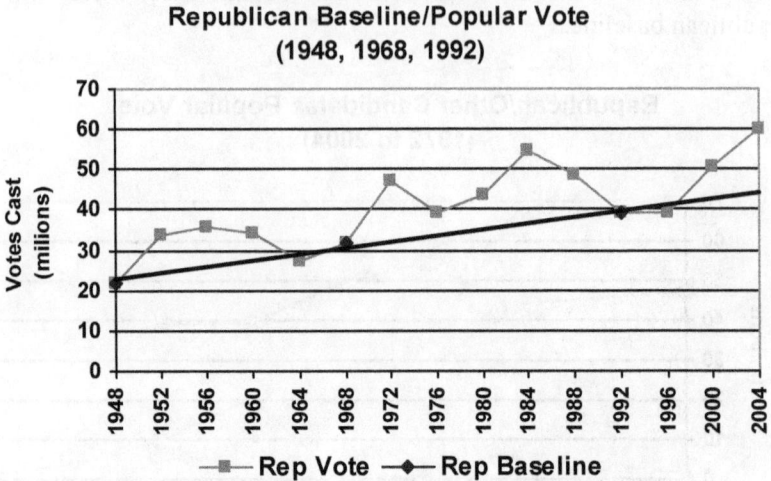

Figure 6-5 - Republican Candidates Baseline Trend
(1948 - 2004)

Source: Dave Leip's Atlas of U.S. Presidential Elections, uselectionatlas.org

The Other Candidates Upper Limit

Unlike the Democrat and Republican baseline trends, the Other candidates' trend does not represent a minimum amount of votes cast. Instead the Other candidates' trend provides a maximum or "upper limit" amount of votes that are obtainable.

As Figure 6-6 displays, the Other candidate votes cast have not been greater than the "upper limit" trend. As a consequence, the Other candidates should never receive more votes than the "upper limit."[66]

_____

[66] Unless a new major realignment of the electorate occurs.

**Other Candidates Upper Limit/Popular Vote
(1948 to 2004)**

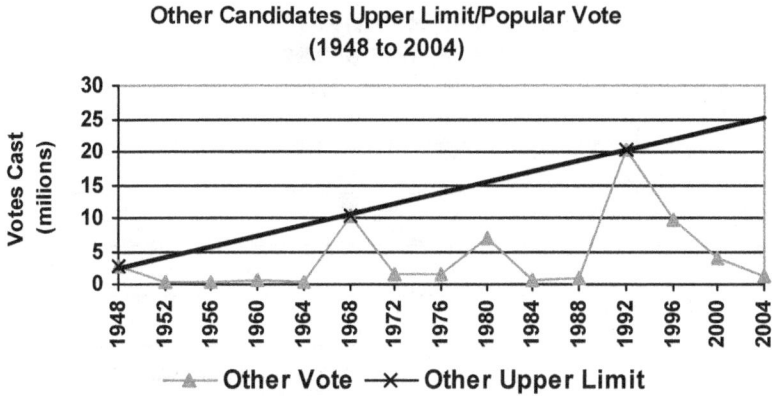

Source: Dave Leip's Atlas of U.S. Presidential Elections, uselectionatlas.org

Figure 6-6 - Other Candidates Upper Limit Trend
(1948 - 2004)

A Non-Democrat Shift in 1972

It stands to reason that a shift in the Democrat baseline from 1968 to 1972 would result in an increase in the Non-Democrat voting electorate. In fact, if we take the graph of Figure 6-2 (Democratic baseline trend with a shift in 1972) and plot the Non-Democrat election points, the Non-Democrat shift becomes apparent. Figure 6-7 clearly displays that from 1968 to 1972 the Democratic Trend "bottoming" out and a corresponding Non-Democrat trend[67] bending upwards. In essence, this presents the last major shift of voters from the Democrat electorate to the Non-Democrat electorate.[68]

---

[67] Since the Non–Democrats include both Republican and Other candidate voters the Trend is an "upper limit" as opposed to a baseline.

[68] The major consequence of these shifts is that slope of the Non–Democrat trend is now lower than the Democratic Trend.

**Democrat/Non-Democrat Trends
(1948, 1968, 1972 & 1992)**

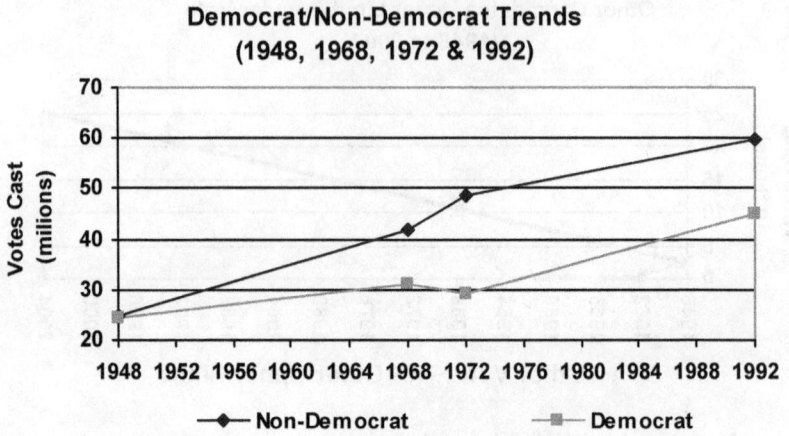

Source: Dave Leip's Atlas of U.S. Presidential Elections, uselectionatlas.org

Figure 6-7 - Non-Democrat/Democrat Trends
(1948, 1968, 1972, and 1992)

PART 2

Trend Analysis

Chapter 7

Proving the Phenomenon

*"Predicting the future is easy. It's trying to figure out
what's going on now that's hard."*

Anonymous

Introduction

In order to prove that the Democratic Trend Phenomenon exists, the
trends should be quantified in some manner. Therefore, numerical values
should be calculated to validate the linearity and thus the predictability of
the popular vote for the Democratic candidate.

Predictable Trend Since 1980

Since the predictable trend, from 1972 to 2004, includes a "deviating"
election in 1976, we will first analyze the segment of the Democratic
Trend that does not include that particular election. Therefore, the
popular vote in each of the presidential elections since 1980 should be
analyzed. Table 7-1 contains the votes cast for the Democrat, Republican,
and Other candidates since 1980. Figure 7-1 presents this data in a bar
chart graphical format.

Table 7-1 - Popular Vote in Presidential Elections
1980 - 2004
(millions)

	'80	'84	'88	'92	'96	'00	'04
Democrat	35.5	37.6	41.8	44.9	47.4	51.0	59.0
Republican	43.9	54.5	48.9	39.1	39.2	50.5	62.0
Other	7.1	0.6	0.9	20.4	9.7	4.0	1.2

Source: Dave Leip's Atlas of U.S. Presidential Elections, uselectionatlas.org

Note: The values have been rounded to the nearest single decimal point.

Figure 7-1 indicates that the popular vote for the Republican and Other candidates have fluctuated up and down since 1980 while the votes for the Democratic candidate have steadily increased. Not only has the popular vote for the Democratic candidate increased in every election since 1980, after a close inspection, it appears to have increased in a linear fashion.

Popular Vote in Presidential Elections (1980 to 2004)

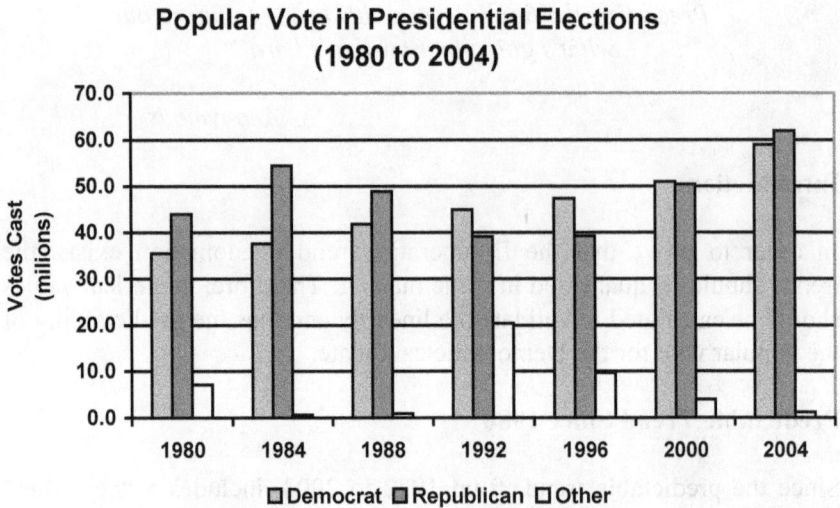

Source: Dave Leip's Atlas of U.S. Presidential Elections, uselectionatlas.org

Figure 7-1 - Popular Vote in Presidential Elections
(1980-2004)

Thus, the popular vote for the Democratic candidate tends to follow along a straight line from election to election. The linear aspect of the popular vote may not be apparent until displayed in a scatter graph format.

For clarity, Figure 7-2 displays a scatter graph of only the votes cast for the Democratic candidate from 1980 to 2004.

By simply glancing at Figure 7-2, the votes cast appear to increase in a linear fashion. However, in order to truly determine if the votes cast are linear we must measure the correlation between the increase in votes cast and the increase in election years. In essence, we need to measure how close the votes cast are to a straight line.

Popular Vote for the Democractic Candidate
(1980 - 2004)

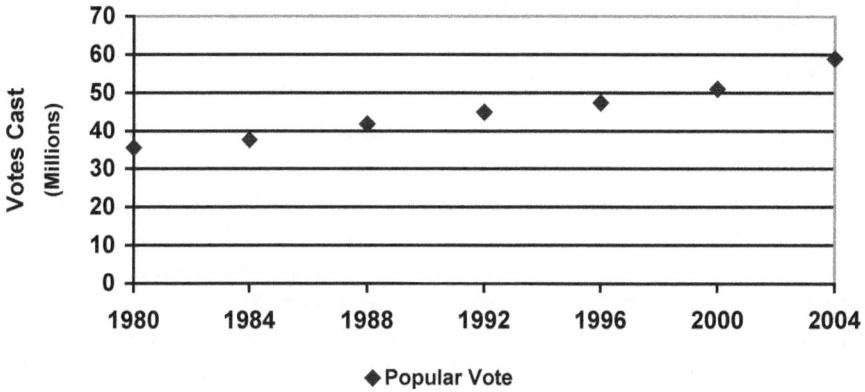

◆ Popular Vote

Source: Dave Leip's Atlas of U.S. Presidential Elections, uselectionatlas.org

Figure 7-2 - Popular Vote of the Democratic Candidate
(1980-2004)

The most common measurement for correlations is called the "Correlation Coefficient." The Correlation Coefficient measures the degree and direction of linear relationship between two variables.[69] The most common Correlation Coefficient is referred to by "r".

Another, and sometimes more useful indicator, is calculated by squaring r. This is called the "Coefficient of Determination" or r^2. The r^2 presents a measurement of the proportion of the variation that one variable can be accounted for by the other. In other words, r^2 measures of how well the regression line represents the data or in this case how well it follows the Democratic Trend line. In this instance, using the votes cast for the Democratic candidate in relationship to the presidential election years from 1980 to 2004, is calculated to be .964. Thus 96.4% of the increase of votes cast is associated with the increase in election year. A Coefficient of Determination of 1.00 or 100% has a perfect positive correlation and follows along a straight line. Since a Coefficient of Determination greater than .8 indicates a strong or high correlation, the

---

[69] A perfect correlation is has an r of 1.00 and an r^2 of 1.00.

votes cast for the Democratic candidate also reflect high correlation. It is important to note that in this particular instance it is not significant that the values be tremendously accurate (ex. .964 or .953). **The most important aspect of this theory is not the specific values of the trend lines but that the popular vote for Democratic candidate for president trended in an extremely predictable pattern for almost thirty years.**

To illustrate how impressively strong this correlation is, compare the same correlation for the popular vote for the Republican and Other candidates. The Coefficient of Determination for the votes cast for the Republican candidate from 1980 to 2004 is calculated to be an unimpressive .115. This means that only 11.5% of the increase of votes cast is associated with the increase in election year. The Coefficient of Determination for the votes cast for the Other candidates is even worse at .00006. This means that only 0.006% of the increase of votes cast is associated with the increase in election year.

A second method of proving the linearity of the election points is to compare the data to a "regression line."[70] The regression line is the closest line that best fits all data points. Before a regression line can be plotted, an equation (regression equation) must be derived. Since the regression line is a straight line, it will appear in the form of the standard equation:

$$\hat{y} = bx + a$$

The variable $\hat{y}$ represents the Votes Cast for the Democratic candidate while x will be the presidential election year. The constant a is the value of y if x is zero.[71] The constant b represents the slope of the line.

---

[70] The Least–Squares method of calculating the regression equation was used.

[71] Since x does not begin with 0 election year, the Y–intercept assumes an election year of 1980 instead of the typical 0.

Using the votes cast along with the election years from 1980 to 2004, the equation [72] that depicts the regression line is determined to be (see Appendix A for the specific formulas used in the calculations):

Popular Vote = 0.9204x - 1788

; where x is the election year.

**Popular Vote for the Democractic Candidate
(1980 - 2004)**

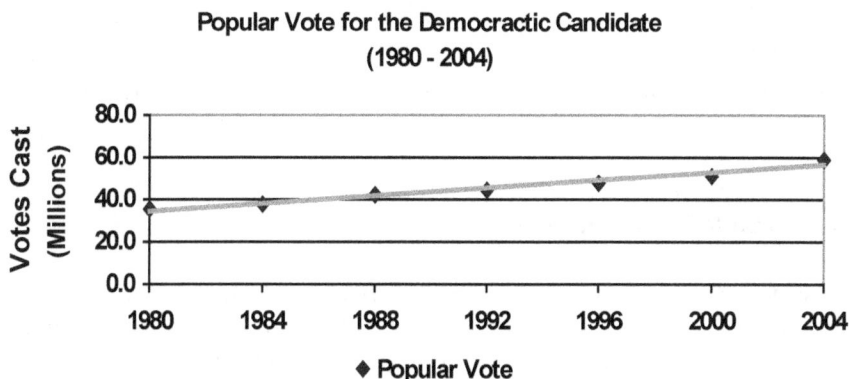

Source: Dave Leip's Atlas of U.S. Presidential Elections, uselectionatlas.org

Figure 7-3 - Popular Vote for the Democratic Candidate
(1980-2004) w/Regression Line

Using the above equation and substituting the appropriate year, estimates of the actual votes cast can be calculated. Table 7-2 displays the results of actual votes cast along with the values calculated using the regression equation. In addition, the accuracy of the estimated votes cast can be calculated to determine the accuracy of the regression line.

The level of accuracy of the estimated value ranges from a maximum of 99.6% to a minimum of 95.5%. With a 96.38% Coefficient of Determination and at least a 95.5% accuracy using the regression equation, it is clear that the votes cast for the Democratic candidate has progressed in a consistent linear trend from 1980 to 2004.

---

[72] The derived equation depends upon the specific popular vote used to calculate the regression line.

Table 7-2 - Popular Vote for the Democratic Candidate and Estimated
Amount, 1980-2004
(millions)

	'80	'84	'88	'92	'96	'00	'04
Democrat	35.5	37.6	41.8	44.9	47.4	51.0	59.0
Estimate ('80-'04)	34.3	37.9	41.6	45.3	48.9	52.6	56.3
Accuracy%	96.6	99.0	99.6	99.1	96.7	96.8	95.6

Source: Dave Leip's Atlas of U.S. Presidential Elections, uselectionatlas.org

Note: The values have been rounded to the nearest single decimal point. See Appendix B for actual values used in the calculations.

Predictable Trend Since 1972

The next step is to prove whether the predictable trend extends to the election of 1972. However, the 1976 election will be removed from the calculations because it has been designated a "deviating" election and will be treated as an outlier.[73]

Table 7-3 - Popular Vote in Presidential Elections,
1972-2004
(millions)

	'72	'76	'80	'84	'88	'92	'96	'00	'04
Democrat	29.2	40.8	35.5	37.6	41.8	44.9	47.4	51.0	59.0
Republican	47.2	39.2	43.9	54.5	48.9	39.1	39.2	50.5	62.0
Other	1.4	1.6	7.1	0.6	0.9	20.4	9.7	4.0	1.2

Source: Dave Leip's Atlas of U.S. Presidential Elections, uselectionatlas.org

As before, we should begin by reviewing the popular vote since 1972 in table and graphical form (see Table 7-3 and Figure 7-4). Figure 7-4 clearly shows that the votes cast for Republican and Other candidates show no obvious consistent trend throughout the elections of 1972 to 2004. However, the votes cast in 1972 for the Democratic candidate appear to be aligned with the elections of 1980 through 2000.

---

[73] Outliers are individual points that are substantial greater or smaller than the other values in a data set. In many instances outliers are eliminated from the data set in order to not skew the analysis.

Popular Vote in Presidential Elections
(1972 to 2004)

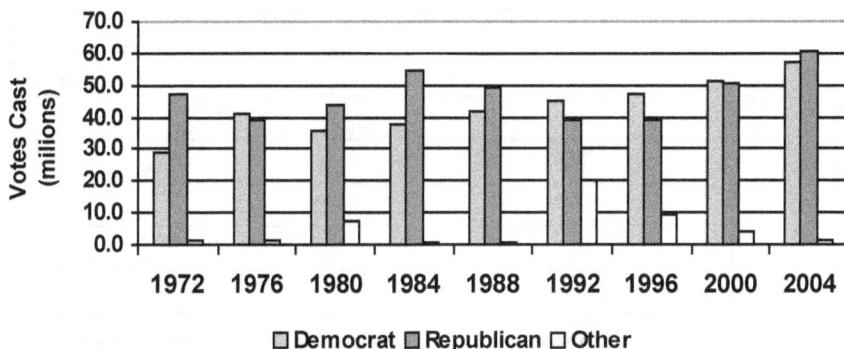

Source: Dave Leip's Atlas of U.S. Presidential Elections, uselectionatlas.org

Figure 7-4 - Presidential Popular Vote (1972-2004)

In fact, recalculating the regression equation for the election years of 1972 to 2004, but excluding 1976, yields similar results as before. The new regression equation for 1972 through 2004 becomes:

Popular Vote = 0.8707x - 1689

; where x is the election year.

Nonetheless, the consistent trend of votes cast can be easily identified in Figure 7-5 when the data is viewed as a line graph compared to the Regression Line.

Table 7-4 includes the results of actual votes cast along with the values calculated using the new regression formula. As before, the deviation between the actual votes cast and the estimated votes cast can be calculated to determine the accuracy of the formula.

Popular Vote for the Democratic Candidate
(1972 - 2004)

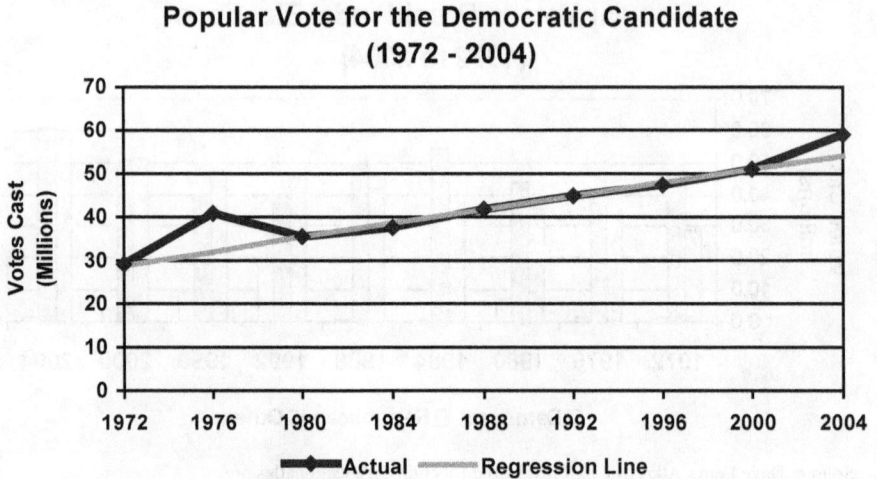

Source: Dave Leip's Atlas of U.S. Presidential Elections, uselectionatlas.org

Figure 7-5 - Popular Vote for the Democratic Candidate
(1972-2004)

Excluding 1976 as an outlier, the highest accuracy between the actual and the regression line, range from a maximum of 99.6% and a low of 94.7%. Therefore, the regression line formula is better than 94.7% accurate.

Table 7-4 - Popular Vote for Democratic Candidate in Presidential Elections
and Predicted Amount, 1972-2004
(millions)

	'72	'80	'84	'88	'92	'96	'00	'04
Democrat	29.2	35.5	37.6	41.8	44.9	47.4	51.0	59.0
Estimate ('72 -'04)	28.1	35.0	38.5	42.0	45.5	48.9	52.4	55.9
Accuracy%	96.3	98.7	97.5	99.6	98.7	96.7	97.2	94.7

Source: Dave Leip's Atlas of U.S. Presidential Elections, uselectionatlas.org

The Coefficient of Determination is calculated to be .973. At 97.3% the Coefficient of Determination for 1972 to 2004 shows a stronger relationship than the one calculated from 1980 to 2004. With such a high correlation, this clearly establishes that since 1972 the popular vote for the Democratic candidate has increased in a predictable trend, with the exception of the 1976 election.

Chapter 8

Predicting the Popular Vote

*"It is a test of true theories not only to account for
but to predict phenomena."*

William Whewell

Introduction

Now that the popular vote for the Democratic candidate has been proven to be linear[74], the essential question still remains; could a projection of future votes cast have been derived? In other words, could the popular vote for the Democratic candidate been predicted prior to the election? This chapter investigates whether the Democratic Trend could have been used to predict the next election four years earlier using the prior popular vote. Thus, we put the Democratic Trend to test or as William Whewell stated, *"It is a test of true theories not only to account for but to predict phenomena."*

Predicting the 1988 Election

In order to make a valid prediction, we require at least three elections. Consequently, the first prediction will have to be the 1988 election. As a result, the regression equation must be derived from using the popular vote in the elections of 1972, 1980, and 1984. When calculated, the regression equation would be:

$$\text{Popular Vote} = 0.7129x - 1377$$

; where x is the election year.

The results obtained by calculating the popular vote for the 1988 election using the above regression equation, is presented in Table 8-1. The estimated votes cast are found to be 97.4% accurate.

---

[74] Increasing along a straight line with a high level of accuracy.

Table 8-1 - Popular Vote for Democratic Candidate
and the Predicted Amount, 1988
(millions)

	1988
Democratic Popular Vote	41.8
Prediction ('72-'84)	40.7
Accuracy%	97.4%

By determining the Coefficient of Determination for the votes cast from 1972, 1980, and 1984 an alternative measurement of the linearity can be made. The Coefficient of Determination, r^2, for the votes cast is calculated to be .9906. Also, the 1992, 1996, 2000, 2004 elections could have predicted with a 97.0%, 98.0%, 96.5%, and 88.3% accuracy.

Predicting the 1992 Election

The next election that could have been predicted would have been the 1992 election. The regression equation derived from using the votes cast in the prior elections of 1972, 1980, 1984, and 1988 would be:

Popular Vote = 0.767x - 1483

; where x is the election year.

The results obtained by calculating the votes cast for the 1992 election using the above regression equation, is presented in Table 8-2. The estimated votes cast are found to be 99.0% accurate.

Table 8-2 - Popular Vote for the Democratic Candidate
and the Predicted Amount, 1992
(millions)

	1992
Democratic Popular Vote	44.9
Prediction ('72-'88)	44.4
Accuracy%	99.0%

The Coefficient of Determination, r^2, for the votes cast from 1972 to 1992 is calculated to be .9940. Also, the 1996, 2000, 2004 elections could have predicted with a 99.7%, 99.1%, and 90.9% accuracy.

Predicting the 1996 Election

The regression equation derived using the popular vote for the elections of 1972, 1980, 1984, 1988, and 1992 would be:

$$\text{Popular Vote} = 0.7841x - 1517$$

; where x is the election year.

The result obtained by calculating the votes cast for the 1996 election using the above regression equation, is presented in Table 8-3. The estimated votes cast is found to be 99.1% accurate.

Table 8-3 - Popular Vote for the Democratic Candidate
and the Predicted Amount, 1996
(millions)

	1996
Democratic Popular Vote	47.4
Prediction ('72-'92)	47.8
%Accuracy	99.1%

The Coefficient of Determination, r^2 for the votes cast from 1972 to 1996 is calculated to be .9956. Also, the 2000 and 2004 elections could have predicted with a 99.9%, and 91.6% accuracy.

Predicting the 2000 Election

Furthermore, the regression equation derived from using the popular vote for the elections of 1972, 1980, 1984, 1988, 1992, and 1996 would be:

$$\text{Popular Vote} = 0.7719x - 1493$$

; where x is the election year.

The result obtained by calculating the votes cast for the 2000 election using the above regression equation, is presented in Table 8-4. The estimated votes cast are found to be 99.43% accurate.

Table 8-4 - Popular Vote for the Democratic Candidate
and the Predicted Amount, 2000
(millions)

	2000
Democratic Popular Vote	51.0
Prediction ('72-'96)	50.7
Accuracy%	99.4%

The Coefficient of Determination, r^2 for the votes cast from 1972 to 2000 is calculated to be .9970. Also, the 2004 elections could have predicted with a 91.1% accuracy.

Predicting the 2004 Election

The regression equation derived from using the popular vote for the elections of 1972, 1980, 1984, 1988, 1992, 1996, and 2000 would be:

Popular Vote = 0.7785x - 1506

; where x is the election year.

The result obtained by calculating the votes cast for the 2004 election using the above regression equation, is presented in Table 8-5. The estimated votes cast are found to be 91.4% accurate.[75]

Table 8-5 - Popular Vote for the Democratic Candidate
and the Predicted Amount, 2004
(millions)

	2004
Democratic Popular Vote	59.0
Prediction ('72-'00)	54.0
%Accuracy	91.4%

As determined in Chapter 7, the Coefficient of Determination, r^2 for the votes cast for the Democratic candidate in relationship to the presidential elections years from 1972 to 2004 is calculated to be .973. Thus the

---

[75] This 2004 estimate is different from the estimate calculated in Table 6-4. Table 6-4 uses the trend lines from 1972 to 2004 instead of 1972 to 2000 as in Table 7-5.

97.3% of the variability of the votes cast can be predicted from the relationship with the election year.

Predictions of the Popular Vote for the Democratic Candidate (1988 - 2004)

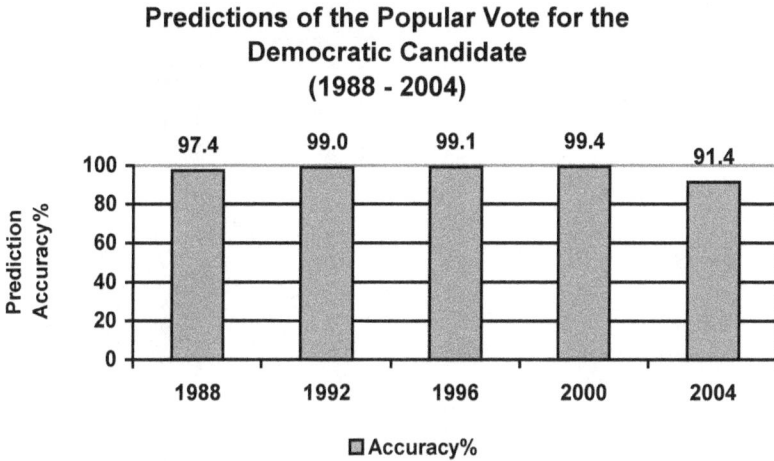

Figure 8-1 - Accuracy of Regression Predictions

Reviewing all of the predictions we can easily conclude that since 1988 accurate projections of the popular vote for the Democratic candidate could have been made. Figure 8-1 presents a graph of the accuracies of the predictions.

Notice that the prediction becomes more accurate with each additional election up to 2000. This is an indication that the Democratic Trend was becoming more linear with each election. However, the accuracy of the 2004 election was less precise than the other four. The cause of this lower accuracy will be discussed in more detail in Chapter 12.

Chapter 9

Analyzing the Baseline Trends

*"It is my deep conviction that we have reached a turning point
in the long history of our efforts to guarantee freedom
and equality to all our citizens."*

Harry S. Truman

Introduction

As discussed in Chapter 6, the elections of 1948, 1968, and 1992 form
the baseline or "upper limit" trends for the Democratic, Republican and
Other or Non-Majority Party candidates' voters. President Truman's
policies and his statements like, *"It is my deep conviction that we have
reached a turning point in the long history of our efforts to guarantee
freedom and equality to all our citizens"* might have contributed to the
first fissure in the electorate and possibly the creation of the
baseline/upper limit trends. This chapter reviews the linearity and
accuracy of the baseline/upper limit trend.

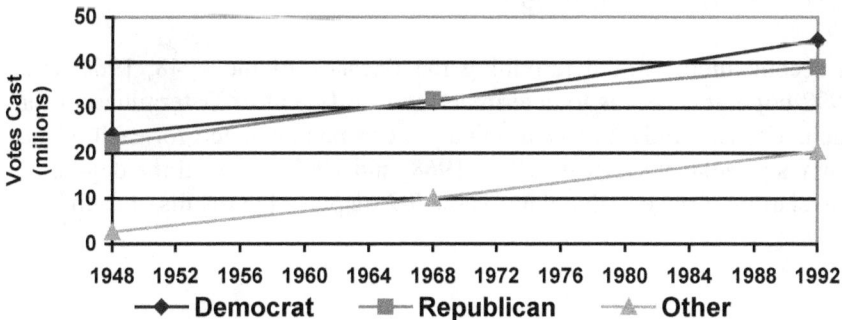

Popular Vote in Presidential Elections
(1948, 1968 & 1992)

Source: Dave Leip's Atlas of U.S. Presidential Elections, uselectionatlas.org

Figure 9-1 - Democrat, Republican, Other Candidates
Popular Vote (1948, 1968 & 1992)

Defining the Baseline/Upper Limit

The regression equations can be developed for each of the baselines. Using the Democrat, Republican and Other votes cast for the election years of 1948, 1968, 1992 the following equations can be derived[76]:

Democrat Baseline Popular Vote = 0.4743x - 901
Republican Baseline Popular Vote = 0.3862x - 730
Other Upper Limit Popular Vote = 0.4050x - 787

; where x is the election year.

Using the above equation and substituting the appropriate year, estimates of the votes cast can be calculated. Table 9-1 displays the results of accuracy of the regression equation for each baseline/upper limit.

Table 9-1 - Accuracy of The Regression Equation
1948, 1968, 1992

	1948	1968	1992
Democrat	96.5%	95.0%	98.4%
Republican	96.7%	95.8%	98.4%
Other	92.2%	96.3%	99.2%

Note: The values have been rounded to the nearest single decimal point. For actual values used in the calculations see Appendix B.

Measuring the Relationship

A second method of determining the linearity of the 1948, 1968, and 1992 popular votes' is to determine the Coefficient of Determination for each. The Coefficient of Determination can be calculated for each of the Party's popular votes from 1948, 1968, and 1992 to reveal the degree of correlation of the election data. Table 9-2 displays the results of each.

---

[76] A Non–Democrat equation can be developed by adding the Republican and Other candidates' equations together to get the Non–Democrats Popular Vote = .7912x – 1516.1.

Table 9-2 - Coefficient of Determination
1948, 1968, 1992

	r^2
Democrat	.9837
Republican	.9817
Other	.9987

As Table 9-2 indicates each of the Party's Coefficient of Determination show a strong relationship. The strong relationship of these three elections for these three electoral Party's represents one thing - each of these baselines/upper limit trend represent a continuation of similar voters from one election to another.

Trend Shift in 1972

As Chapter 6 discusses, there was a change in the Democrat baseline trend in 1972. The Democrat baseline dipped lower from 1968 to 1972 and thus now follows the Democratic Trend line from 1972 to 2004. However, the reverse is assumed for the Non-Democrat trend. The Non-Democrat trend combines both the Republican baseline and the Other candidates upper limit. Also, since the Republican and Other candidates are vying for the same voters, combining the trends creates an "upper limit" and not a "baseline." Thus, the Non-Democrat "upper limit" Trend depicts the highest amount of votes that Republicans or Other candidates can obtain.

To illustrate, Figure 9-2 shows that from 1968 to 1972 the Democratic Trend dips downward while a corresponding Non-Democrat trend bends upward. This changes the path and equation of each trend. After the shift in 1972, the Democratic baseline coincides with the existing Democratic Trend. Nevertheless, the Non-Democrat trend should reflect a mirroring adjustment to the Democratic must be recalculated using the two election points of 1972 and 1992. Using the two election points the new equation is determined to be:

Non-Democrat Max Popular Vote = 0.7919x - 1516.1

; where x is the election year.

Democrat/Non-Democrat Popular Vote
(1948, 1968, 1972 & 1992)

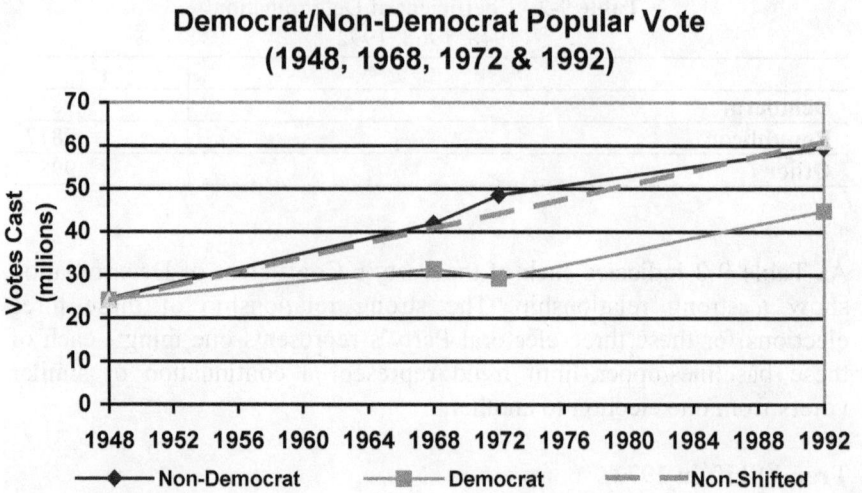

Source: Dave Leip's Atlas of U.S. Presidential Elections, uselectionatlas.org

Figure 9-2 - Shifted Non-Democrat/Democrat Trends
(1948, 1968, 1972, and 1992)

The effect of the shifted Non-Democrat trend appears to be minor between the years of 1972 to 1992. However in the outward years, the shifted trend moves further and further from the non-shifted trend and closer to the Democrat trend line. Chapters 12 discuss the future implications of this shift on the Democrat and Non-Democrat electorate.

PART 3

The State Trend

Chapter 10

Analyzing the Trend State by State

"In politics, like geometry, the whole
is equal to the sum of its parts."

A. Fairfax

Introduction

Intuitively, it stands to reason that if the national popular vote for the Democratic candidate has been increasing in a predictable trend since 1972, then this pattern should exist in one or more states.[77] The only other alternative to this hypothesis is a scenario whereby each election includes a different group of voters in one state that compensate exactly for another group in another state. This circumstance would have to occur in order to form a linear trend at the national level. Of course this latter scenario is not likely.

What is a likely scenario is that there exist a majority of states that contain a similar trend to the one displayed nationally.[78] This chapter reviews the correlations for each state.

Predictable Trend at the State Level

There are several obstacles that occur with the trend existing at the state level. First, the population of the state is less stable than the country. That is to say, individuals move from state to state but usually stay inside the country. Second, the old axiom by Speaker of the House Tip O'neil is true: *"All Politics is local."*

---

[77] The trend or pattern should also manifest itself at the county level.

[78] In fact, using the elections of 1972 to 2004 and excluding the 1976 election, 84% of the country's voting age population resides in states with a Democratic Coefficient of Determination (r^2) of greater than .81 (a very strong correlation coefficient (r) of greater than .9).

Locally, the turnout will vary along with different state referendum issues and campaigns. For example, controversial state referendums may have the effect of increasing the turnout for or against. The combination of these two factors should yield a condition where the Democratic Trend Phenomenon will not be as consistent at the state level as existed at the national level. Consequently, the very existence of the Democratic Trend Phenomenon at the state level is much more impressive than the existence at the national level.

Table 10-1 - State Coefficient of Determination for Democratic
Candidates for President
$(1972 - 2004)^{79}$

State	R^2	State	r^2
Virginia	0.972392	Indiana	0.848034
Vermont	0.958105	Georgia	0.846570
Maryland	0.955123	Delaware	0.833371
Florida	0.954477	Utah	0.831869
Washington	0.954441	Tennessee	0.831125
Arizona	0.952427	Idaho	0.829593
Hawaii	0.941847	Minnesota	0.820835
New Mexico	0.937210	Pennsylvania	0.813496
New Jersey	0.933067	Wisconsin	0.804905
Maine	0.931146	Kansas	0.787281
North Carolina	0.930285	Oklahoma	0.774954
Texas	0.901070	Kentucky	0.727466
Connecticut	0.900664	Iowa	0.713990
Colorado	0.900608	Louisiana	0.682415
Alaska	0.899333	Alabama	0.660415
Illinois	0.897701	Massachusetts	0.659059
Missouri	0.895865	Nebraska	0.658229
California	0.890153	Wyoming	0.650584
Oregon	0.888841	Arkansas	0.646334
New York	0.881512	D.C.	0.586602
South Carolina	0.881287	Mississippi	0.549828
New Hampshire	0.879574	Montana	0.499424
Michigan	0.866898	South Dakota	0.077670
Rhode Island	0.859028	North Dakota	0.072196
Ohio	0.858777	West Virginia	0.004262
Nevada	0.857386		

[79] Excluding the election of 1976.

Nonetheless, verifying the Democratic Trend Phenomenon can be achieved by using the same techniques that were used at the national level. Thus, determining the linearity of the popular vote using the Coefficient of Determination (r^2) will be the first step in verifying a predictable trend. Table 10-1 displays the states' Coefficient of Determination for the popular vote of the Democratic candidate for the elections from 1972 to 2004 (excluding 1976).

Table 10-2 - State Coefficient of Determination for Republican
Candidates for President
$(1972 - 2004)$[80]

State	R^2	State	R^2
Alaska	0.772220	Louisiana	0.235197
Nevada	0.726159	Mississippi	0.231232
South Carolina	0.702156	Massachusetts	0.220121
D.C.	0.690983	Minnesota	0.219966
Arizona	0.674109	Wisconsin	0.184295
Georgia	0.656186	Montana	0.157166
North Carolina	0.629555	West Virginia	0.151903
Virginia	0.602409	Maryland	0.076671
Alabama	0.567065	Nebraska	0.061283
Florida	0.552972	South Dakota	0.055617
Texas	0.536691	Pennsylvania	0.045050
New York	0.505964	Kansas	0.043813
Tennessee	0.505209	Iowa	0.037104
Colorado	0.454449	North Dakota	0.036809
Idaho	0.419631	Indiana	0.035012
Rhode Island	0.406165	Missouri	0.024115
Oregon	0.385464	Arkansas	0.021653
Illinois	0.379359	Delaware	0.020216
Utah	0.365817	Oklahoma	0.019872
Connecticut	0.359908	Maine	0.012105
Kentucky	0.328352	Vermont	0.007157
Washington	0.317352	Hawaii	0.002314
New Jersey	0.303119	Ohio	0.001273
Wyoming	0.297184	Michigan	0.000170
New Mexico	0.239209	California	0.000154
New Hampshire	0.237078		

---

[80] Excluding the election of 1976.

It is important to mention that a Coefficient of Determination that is greater than .81 shows very high linear correlation. As Table 10-1 indicates there are 34 states that have a Coefficient of Determination that is greater than .81. Only four (4) states have a Coefficient of Determination that is less than .50. In fact a majority of states (26) have a Coefficient of Determination of greater than .85.

Alternately, Table 10-2 presents the Coefficient of Determination for the Republican candidates for the election of 1972 to 2004. Table 10-2 shows that there are no states that have a Coefficient of Determination above .81. Furthermore, there are 38 states with a Coefficient of Determination under .50. This equates to more than nine times the amount of the Democratic Trend.

Virginia - A Mini Democratic Trend Phenomenon

At the top of the states is Virginia, showing the highest similarity with the national Democratic Trend Phenomenon.[81] With a Coefficient of Determination of approximately .9724, Virginia seems to almost mimic the national trend. The value was .9738 nationally (see Chapter 7 - A predictable Trend Since 1972). Below outlines the similar trend statistics and formulas that were used to analyze the national phenomenon in Chapters 7 through 9.

Coefficient of Determination:
Democrat = 0.972392
Republican = 0.602409

Democrat Popular Vote = .02891x - 56.556

---

[81] Using the elections of 1972 through 2004, excluding 1976.

Table 10-3 - Virginia Popular Vote for the Democratic Candidate, 1972-2004 (millions)

	1972	1980	1984	1988	1992	1996	2000	2004
Democrat	0.44	0.75	0.80	0.86	1.04	1.09	1.22	1.45
Prediction	0.45	0.68	0.80	0.91	1.03	1.14	1.26	1.38
Accuracy%	97.4	90.6	99.9	93.8	99.0	95.1	96.5	94.5

Source: Dave Leip's Atlas of U.S. Presidential Elections, uselectionatlas.org

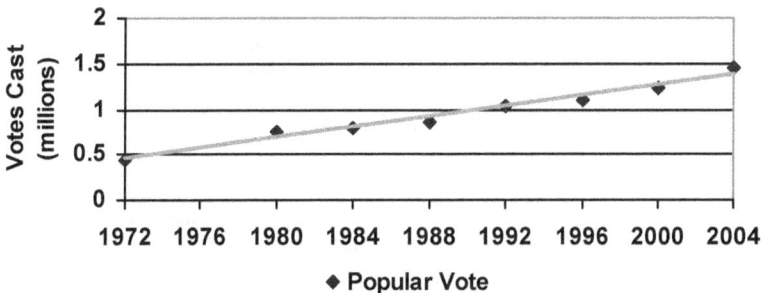

Virginia Democratic Popular Vote (1972-2004)

Source: Dave Leip's Atlas of U.S. Presidential Elections, uselectionatlas.org

Figure 10-1 Virginia Popular Vote for Democratic Candidates (1972-2004)

The Mirror Phenomenon in Virginia

As presented in Chapter 4, the fracturing of the electorate in 1968 caused a unique mirroring phenomenon between the Republican and Other or Non-Majority Party candidates' popular votes. If the Democratic Trend exists at the state level there must be a similar mirror phenomenon for the states as well. This turns out to be true.

Virginia possesses one of the leading examples of the mirror effect for Republican and Other candidates votes cast. Figure 10-2 presents the Republican as well as the Other candidates popular vote for the elections from 1972 to 2004 (excluding 1976). As with Figure 4-2 in Chapter 5, the Republican votes cast decrease when the Other candidates performs well. Conversely, the Other candidates votes cast decrease when the Republican performs well. The net effect is a mirror image.

Virginia Republican/Other Popular Vote
(1972-2004)

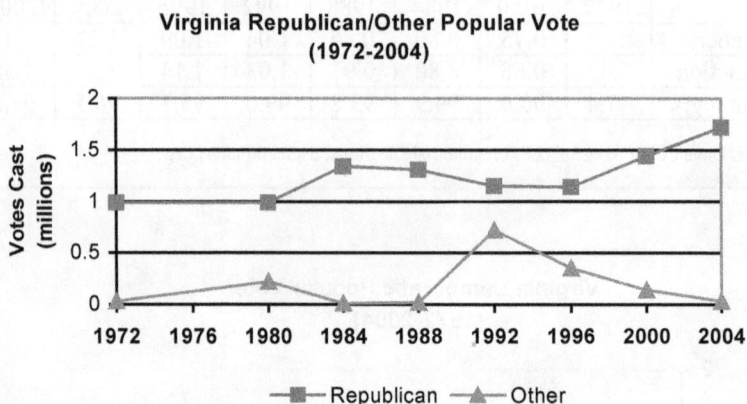

Source: Dave Leip's Atlas of U.S. Presidential Elections, uselectionatlas.org

Figure 10-2 Virginia Republican/Other Popular Vote
(1972-2004)

It turns out that the mirror image for Virginia is just as symmetrical as the one depicted at the national level.

Democratic Trend in Other States

The next several pages presents a brief snapshot of the remaining states sorted by their Coefficient of Determination for the Democratic candidate. Included for each state are the following: Coefficient of Determination for the Democrat and Republican candidates; regression equation to estimate the popular vote for the Democratic candidate (in millions); and a table listing the vote for the Democratic candidate for the elections of 1972 - 2004 (excluding 1976) plus the accuracy of the regression equation.

Vermont

Coefficient of Determination (R-squared):
Democrat = 0.958905
Republican = 0.007169

Democrat Popular Vote = .00350x - 6.8425

;where "x" is the election year.

Year	1972	1980	1984	1988	1992	1996	2000	2004
Democrat	0.07	0.08	0.10	0.12	0.13	0.14	0.15	0.18
Prediction	0.06	0.09	0.10	0.12	0.13	0.14	0.16	0.17
Accuracy%	87.3	93.1	94.0	99.8	97.0	95.9	94.3	93.2

Source: Dave Leip's Atlas of U.S. Presidential Elections, uselectionatlas.org

---

Maryland

Coefficient of Determination (R-squared):
Democrat = 0.955097
Republican = 0.076682

Democrat Popular Vote = .02357x - 45.984

;where "x" is the election year.

Year	1972	1980	1984	1988	1992	1996	2000	2004
Democrat	0.51	0.73	0.79	0.83	0.99	0.97	1.15	1.33
Prediction	0.50	0.69	0.78	0.87	0.97	1.06	1.16	1.25
Accuracy%	98.4	94.5	99.1	94.1	98.0	89.9	99.0	93.8

Source: Dave Leip's Atlas of U.S. Presidential Elections, uselectionatlas.org

Florida

Coefficient of Determination (R-squared):
Democrat = 0.954478
Republican = 0.552971

Democrat Popular Vote = .08493x - 166.92

;where "x" is the election year.

Year	1972	1980	1984	1988	1992	1996	2000	2004
Democrat	0.72	1.42	1.45	1.66	2.07	2.55	2.91	3.58
Prediction	0.56	1.24	1.58	1.92	2.26	2.60	2.94	3.28
Accuracy%	77.8	87.2	91.1	84.3	91.1	98.0	99.2	91.4

Source: Dave Leip's Atlas of U.S. Presidential Elections, uselectionatlas.org

---

Washington

Coefficient of Determination (R-squared):
Democrat = 0.954439
Republican = 0.317365

Democrat Popular Vote = .02860x - 55.911

;where "x" is the election year.

Year	1972	1980	1984	1988	1992	1996	2000	2004
Democrat	0.57	0.65	0.81	0.93	0.99	1.12	1.25	1.51
Prediction	0.48	0.71	0.82	0.94	1.05	1.17	1.28	1.39
Accuracy%	84.2	91.2	98.2	99.7	94.2	96.3	97.5	92.3

Source: Dave Leip's Atlas of U.S. Presidential Elections, uselectionatlas.org

Arizona

Coefficient of Determination (R-squared):
Democrat = 0.952441
Republican = 0.674123

Democrat Popular Vote = .02183x - 42.928

;where "x" is the election year.

Year	1972	1980	1984	1988	1992	1996	2000	2004
Democrat	0.20	0.25	0.33	0.45	0.54	0.65	0.69	0.89
Prediction	0.12	0.29	0.38	0.47	0.56	0.64	0.73	0.82
Accuracy%	60.0	81.0	85.9	96.9	97.7	98.4	93.4	91.5

Source: Dave Leip's Atlas of U.S. Presidential Elections, uselectionatlas.org

---

Hawaii

Coefficient of Determination (R-squared):
Democrat = 0.940587
Republican = 0.002309

Democrat Popular Vote = .00393x - 7.6360

;where "x" is the election year.

Year	1972	1980	1984	1988	1992	1996	2000	2004
Democrat	0.10	0.14	0.15	0.19	0.18	0.21	0.21	0.23
Prediction	0.11	0.14	0.15	0.17	0.18	0.20	0.22	0.23
Accuracy%	95.4	98.8	95.9	87.8	97.1	97.7	94.8	100.0

Source: Dave Leip's Atlas of U.S. Presidential Elections, uselectionatlas.org

New Mexico

Coefficient of Determination (R-squared):
Democrat = 0.937213
Republican = 0.239187

Democrat Popular Vote = .00662x - 12.925

;where "x" is the election year.

Year	1972	1980	1984	1988	1992	1996	2000	2004
Democrat	0.14	0.17	0.20	0.24	0.26	0.27	0.29	0.37
Prediction	0.13	0.18	0.21	0.23	0.26	0.29	0.31	0.34
Accuracy%	90.5	92.4	97.4	95.5	99.4	95.2	90.9	91.5

Source: Dave Leip's Atlas of U.S. Presidential Elections, uselectionatlas.org

---

New Jersey

Coefficient of Determination (R-squared):
Democrat = 0.933042
Republican = 0.303115

Democrat Popular Vote = .02722x - 52.706

;where "x" is the election year.

Year	1972	1980	1984	1988	1992	1996	2000	2004
Democrat	1.10	1.15	1.26	1.32	1.44	1.65	1.79	1.91
Prediction	0.98	1.19	1.30	1.41	1.52	1.63	1.74	1.85
Accuracy%	88.6	95.9	96.7	93.1	94.1	98.6	97.2	96.6

Source: Dave Leip's Atlas of U.S. Presidential Elections, uselectionatlas.org

Maine

Coefficient of Determination (R-squared):
Democrat = 0.931444
Republican = 0.012100

Democrat Popular Vote = .00671x - 13.073

;where "x" is the election year.

Year	1972	1980	1984	1988	1992	1996	2000	2004
Democrat	0.16	0.22	0.21	0.24	0.26	0.31	0.32	0.40
Prediction	0.15	0.20	0.23	0.26	0.28	0.31	0.34	0.36
Accuracy%	92.9	91.8	92.9	94.7	92.4	99.2	94.7	91.7

Source: Dave Leip's Atlas of U.S. Presidential Elections, uselectionatlas.org

---

North Carolina

Coefficient of Determination (R-squared):
Democrat = 0.930283
Republican = 0.629548

Democrat Popular Vote = .02939x - 57.463

;where "x" is the election year.

Year	1972	1980	1984	1988	1992	1996	2000	2004
Democrat	0.44	0.88	0.82	0.89	1.11	1.11	1.26	1.53
Prediction	0.49	0.73	0.84	0.96	1.08	1.20	1.31	1.43
Accuracy%	88.3	82.8	97.8	92.1	96.7	92.1	95.6	93.7

Source: Dave Leip's Atlas of U.S. Presidential Elections, uselectionatlas.org

Alaska

Coefficient of Determination (R-squared):
Democrat = 0.901508
Republican = 0.771500

Democrat Popular Vote = .00217x - 4.2514

;where "x" is the election year.

Year	1972	1980	1984	1988	1992	1996	2000	2004
Democrat	0.03	0.04	0.06	0.07	0.08	0.08	0.08	0.11
Prediction	0.03	0.05	0.06	0.07	0.08	0.08	0.09	0.10
Accuracy%	96.3	82.6	93.2	91.6	96.0	95.7	82.9	91.2

Source: Dave Leip's Atlas of U.S. Presidential Elections, uselectionatlas.org

---

Texas

Coefficient of Determination (R-squared):
Democrat = 0.901074
Republican = 0.536692

Democrat Popular Vote = .04511x - 87.584

;where "x" is the election year.

Year	1972	1980	1984	1988	1992	1996	2000	2004
Democrat	1.15	1.88	1.95	2.35	2.28	2.46	2.43	2.83
Prediction	1.38	1.74	1.92	2.10	2.28	2.46	2.64	2.82
Accuracy%	80.6	92.5	98.5	89.3	100.0	99.9	91.4	99.6

Source: Dave Leip's Atlas of U.S. Presidential Elections, uselectionatlas.org

Colorado

Coefficient of Determination (R-squared):
Democrat = 0.900601
Republican = 0.454471

Democrat Popular Vote = .01943x - 38.062

;where "x" is the election year.

Year	1972	1980	1984	1988	1992	1996	2000	2004
Democrat	0.33	0.37	0.45	0.62	0.63	0.67	0.74	1.00
Prediction	0.26	0.42	0.50	0.57	0.65	0.73	0.81	0.88
Accuracy%	79.3	86.6	91.2	92.2	96.7	91.5	90.8	88.2

Source: Dave Leip's Atlas of U.S. Presidential Elections, uselectionatlas.org

---

Connecticut

Coefficient of Determination (R-squared):
Democrat = 0.900589
Republican = 0.359914

Democrat Popular Vote = .01062x - 20.449

;where "x" is the election year.

Year	1972	1980	1984	1988	1992	1996	2000	2004
Democrat	0.56	0.54	0.57	0.68	0.68	0.74	0.82	0.86
Prediction	0.49	0.58	0.62	0.66	0.71	0.75	0.79	0.83
Accuracy%	88.8	93.2	91.0	98.1	96.5	98.3	96.9	97.2

Source: Dave Leip's Atlas of U.S. Presidential Elections, uselectionatlas.org

Illinois

Coefficient of Determination (R-squared):
Democrat = 0.897718
Republican = 0.379358

Democrat Popular Vote = .02927x - 55.926

;where "x" is the election year.

Year	1972	1980	1984	1988	1992	1996	2000	2004
Democrat	1.91	1.98	2.09	2.22	2.45	2.34	2.59	2.89
Prediction	1.80	2.03	2.15	2.27	2.38	2.50	2.62	2.73
Accuracy%	93.9	97.5	97.0	97.8	97.1	93.3	98.9	94.5

Source: Dave Leip's Atlas of U.S. Presidential Elections, uselectionatlas.org

Missouri

Coefficient of Determination (R-squared):
Democrat = 0.895820
Republican = 0.024117

Democrat Popular Vote = .01502x - 28.897

;where "x" is the election year.

Year	1972	1980	1984	1988	1992	1996	2000	2004
Democrat	0.70	0.93	0.85	1.00	1.05	1.03	1.11	1.26
Prediction	0.73	0.85	0.91	0.97	1.03	1.09	1.15	1.21
Accuracy%	95.7	91.1	92.9	96.7	97.6	93.9	96.6	96.0

Source: Dave Leip's Atlas of U.S. Presidential Elections, uselectionatlas.org

California

Coefficient of Determination (R-squared):
Democrat = 0.890154
Republican = 0.000154

Democrat Popular Vote = .10863x - 211.36

;where "x" is the election year.

Year	1972	1980	1984	1988	1992	1996	2000	2004
Democrat	3.48	3.08	3.92	4.70	5.12	5.12	5.86	6.75
Prediction	2.85	3.72	4.16	4.59	5.03	5.46	5.89	6.33
Accuracy%	82.1	79.3	94.0	97.6	98.1	93.4	99.4	93.8

Source: Dave Leip's Atlas of U.S. Presidential Elections, uselectionatlas.org

---

Oregon

Coefficient of Determination (R-squared):
Democrat = 0.888834
Republican = 0.385500

Democrat Popular Vote = .01495x - 29.118

;where "x" is the election year.

Year	1972	1980	1984	1988	1992	1996	2000	2004
Democrat	0.39	0.46	0.54	0.62	0.62	0.65	0.72	0.94
Prediction	0.36	0.48	0.53	0.59	0.65	0.71	0.77	0.83
Accuracy%	90.5	96.0	99.7	96.5	94.7	90.1	92.5	88.4

Source: Dave Leip's Atlas of U.S. Presidential Elections, uselectionatlas.org

New York

Coefficient of Determination (R-squared):
Democrat = 0.881509
Republican = 0.505964

Democrat Popular Vote = .04884x - 93.694

;where "x" is the election year.

Year	1972	1980	1984	1988	1992	1996	2000	2004
Democrat	2.95	2.73	3.12	3.35	3.44	3.76	4.11	4.31
Prediction	2.62	3.01	3.20	3.40	3.59	3.79	3.98	4.18
Accuracy%	88.7	89.8	97.3	98.5	95.7	99.1	97.0	96.9

Source: Dave Leip's Atlas of U.S. Presidential Elections, uselectionatlas.org

---

South Carolina

Coefficient of Determination (R-squared):
Democrat = 0.881333
Republican = 0.702212

Democrat Popular Vote = .01277x - 24.959

;where "x" is the election year.

Year	1972	1980	1984	1988	1992	1996	2000	2004
Democrat	0.19	0.43	0.34	0.37	0.48	0.50	0.57	0.66
Prediction	0.22	0.32	0.37	0.42	0.47	0.53	0.58	0.63
Accuracy%	84.1	75.2	91.8	85.7	99.0	95.7	98.1	94.9

Source: Dave Leip's Atlas of U.S. Presidential Elections, uselectionatlas.org

New Hampshire

Coefficient of Determination (R-squared):
Democrat = 0.879800
Republican = 0.237231

Democrat Popular Vote = .00737x - 14.456

;where "x" is the election year.

Year	1972	1980	1984	1988	1992	1996	2000	2004
Democrat	0.12	0.11	0.12	0.16	0.21	0.25	0.27	0.34
Prediction	0.07	0.13	0.16	0.19	0.21	0.24	0.27	0.30
Accuracy%	58.1	83.8	70.5	86.8	97.2	99.2	97.2	89.1

Source: Dave Leip's Atlas of U.S. Presidential Elections, uselectionatlas.org

---

Michigan

Coefficient of Determination (R-squared):
Democrat = 0.866897
Republican = 0.000170

Democrat Popular Vote = .03020x - 58.222

;where "x" is the election year.

Year	1972	1980	1984	1988	1992	1996	2000	2004
Democrat	1.46	1.66	1.53	1.68	1.87	1.99	2.17	2.48
Prediction	1.33	1.57	1.69	1.81	1.93	2.05	2.17	2.29
Accuracy%	90.9	94.4	89.6	92.0	96.9	96.9	99.9	92.5

Source: Dave Leip's Atlas of U.S. Presidential Elections, uselectionatlas.org

Rhode Island

Coefficient of Determination (R-squared):
Democrat = 0.861474
Republican = 0.406697

Democrat Popular Vote = .00216x - 4.0720

;where "x" is the election year.

Year	1972	1980	1984	1988	1992	1996	2000	2004
Democrat	0.19	0.20	0.20	0.23	0.21	0.23	0.25	0.26
Prediction	0.18	0.20	0.21	0.22	0.23	0.24	0.24	0.25
Accuracy%	94.3	98.7	93.7	96.9	93.7	99.0	97.8	97.3

Source: Dave Leip's Atlas of U.S. Presidential Elections, uselectionatlas.org

---

Ohio

Coefficient of Determination (R-squared):
Democrat = 0.858777
Republican = 0.001273

Democrat Popular Vote = .03102x - 59.687

;where "x" is the election year.

Year	1972	1980	1984	1988	1992	1996	2000	2004
Democrat	1.56	1.75	1.83	1.94	1.98	2.15	2.19	2.74
Prediction	1.47	1.72	1.85	1.97	2.09	2.22	2.34	2.47
Accuracy%	94.6	98.3	98.8	98.4	94.5	96.7	92.8	90.0

Source: Dave Leip's Atlas of U.S. Presidential Elections, uselectionatlas.org

Nevada

Coefficient of Determination (R-squared):
Democrat = 0.857366
Republican = 0.726180

Democrat Popular Vote = .01003x - 19.780

;where "x" is the election year.

Year	1972	1980	1984	1988	1992	1996	2000	2004
Democrat	0.07	0.07	0.09	0.13	0.19	0.20	0.28	0.40
Prediction	0.00	0.08	0.12	0.16	0.20	0.24	0.28	0.32
Accuracy%	4.5	75.4	65.6	76.9	92.4	80.6	98.7	81.5

Source: Dave Leip's Atlas of U.S. Presidential Elections, uselectionatlas.org

---

Indiana

Coefficient of Determination (R-squared):
Democrat = 0.847972
Republican = 0.035014

Democrat Popular Vote = .00636x - 11.788

;where "x" is the election year.

Year	1972	1980	1984	1988	1992	1996	2000	2004
Democrat	0.71	0.84	0.84	0.86	0.85	0.89	0.90	0.97
Prediction	0.75	0.80	0.82	0.85	0.87	0.90	0.92	0.95
Accuracy%	94.6	94.4	97.8	98.6	97.0	98.7	97.5	98.0

Source: Dave Leip's Atlas of U.S. Presidential Elections, uselectionatlas.org

Georgia

Coefficient of Determination (R-squared):
Democrat = 0.846576
Republican = 0.656179

Democrat Popular Vote = .02809x - 54.990

;where "x" is the election year.

Year	1972	1980	1984	1988	1992	1996	2000	2004
Democrat	0.29	0.89	0.71	0.71	1.01	1.05	1.12	1.37
Prediction	0.40	0.63	0.74	0.85	0.96	1.08	1.19	1.30
Accuracy%	61.2	70.3	95.4	80.9	95.5	97.9	93.5	95.2

Source: Dave Leip's Atlas of U.S. Presidential Elections, uselectionatlas.org

---

Delaware

Coefficient of Determination (R-squared):
Democrat = 0.833096
Republican = 0.020252

Democrat Popular Vote = .00336x - 6.5469

;where "x" is the election year.

Year	1972	1980	1984	1988	1992	1996	2000	2004
Democrat	0.09	0.11	0.10	0.11	0.13	0.14	0.18	0.20
Prediction	0.07	0.10	0.11	0.13	0.14	0.15	0.17	0.18
Accuracy%	79.3	94.5	88.5	83.3	88.7	90.5	92.8	90.2

Source: Dave Leip's Atlas of U.S. Presidential Elections, uselectionatlas.org

Utah

Coefficient of Determination (R-squared):
Democrat = 0.832252
Republican = 0.365806

Democrat Popular Vote = .00373x - 7.2281

;where "x" is the election year.

Year	1972	1980	1984	1988	1992	1996	2000	2004
Democrat	0.13	0.12	0.16	0.21	0.18	0.22	0.20	0.24
Prediction	0.12	0.15	0.16	0.18	0.19	0.21	0.22	0.24
Accuracy%	93.2	81.4	95.5	85.5	95.3	93.4	90.7	98.2

Source: Dave Leip's Atlas of U.S. Presidential Elections, uselectionatlas.org

---

Tennessee

Coefficient of Determination (R-squared):
Democrat = 0.831106
Republican = 0.505220

Democrat Popular Vote = .01874x - 36.484

;where "x" is the election year.

Year	1972	1980	1984	1988	1992	1996	2000	2004
Democrat	0.36	0.78	0.71	0.68	0.93	0.91	0.98	1.04
Prediction	0.47	0.62	0.70	0.77	0.85	0.92	1.00	1.07
Accuracy%	68.1	79.3	97.8	86.6	90.6	98.7	98.6	96.7

Source: Dave Leip's Atlas of U.S. Presidential Elections, uselectionatlas.org

Idaho

Coefficient of Determination (R-squared):
Democrat = 0.828829
Republican = 0.419710

Democrat Popular Vote = .00278x - 5.4032

;where "x" is the election year.

Year	1972	1980	1984	1988	1992	1996	2000	2004
Democrat	0.08	0.11	0.11	0.15	0.14	0.17	0.14	0.18
Prediction	0.08	0.11	0.12	0.13	0.14	0.15	0.16	0.17
Accuracy%	94.9	97.3	91.0	87.9	97.4	91.7	82.6	96.1

Source: Dave Leip's Atlas of U.S. Presidential Elections, uselectionatlas.org

---

Minnesota

Coefficient of Determination (R-squared):
Democrat = 0.820806
Republican = 0.219961

Democrat Popular Vote = .01577x - 30.294

;where "x" is the election year.

Year	1972	1980	1984	1988	1992	1996	2000	2004
Democrat	0.80	0.95	1.04	1.11	1.02	1.12	1.17	1.45
Prediction	0.81	0.93	1.00	1.06	1.12	1.18	1.25	1.31
Accuracy%	99.5	97.7	96.0	95.4	90.2	94.3	93.2	90.7

Source: Dave Leip's Atlas of U.S. Presidential Elections, uselectionatlas.org

Pennsylvania

Coefficient of Determination (R-squared):
Democrat = 0.813496
Republican = 0.045052

Democrat Popular Vote = .02921x - 55.849

;where "x" is the election year.

Year	1972	1980	1984	1988	1992	1996	2000	2004
Democrat	1.80	1.94	2.23	2.19	2.24	2.22	2.49	2.94
Prediction	1.74	1.98	2.09	2.21	2.33	2.44	2.56	2.68
Accuracy%	97.0	98.0	94.0	99.3	96.1	89.7	97.0	91.1

Source: Dave Leip's Atlas of U.S. Presidential Elections, uselectionatlas.org

---

Wisconsin

Coefficient of Determination (R-squared):
Democrat = 0.804928
Republican = 0.184298

Democrat Popular Vote = .01698x - 32.685

;where "x" is the election year.

Year	1972	1980	1984	1988	1992	1996	2000	2004
Democrat	0.81	0.98	1.00	1.13	1.04	1.07	1.24	1.49
Prediction	0.80	0.93	1.00	1.07	1.14	1.21	1.27	1.34
Accuracy%	98.5	95.1	99.4	94.9	90.7	87.6	97.6	90.0

Source: Dave Leip's Atlas of U.S. Presidential Elections, uselectionatlas.org

Kansas

Coefficient of Determination (R-squared):
Democrat = 0.787273
Republican = 0.043800

Democrat Popular Vote = .00464x - 8.8567

;where "x" is the election year.

Year	1972	1980	1984	1988	1992	1996	2000	2004
Democrat	0.27	0.33	0.33	0.42	0.39	0.39	0.40	0.43
Prediction	0.29	0.33	0.35	0.36	0.38	0.40	0.42	0.44
Accuracy%	92.9	99.9	96.4	86.0	97.9	96.6	95.0	99.4

Source: Dave Leip's Atlas of U.S. Presidential Elections, uselectionatlas.org

---

Oklahoma

Coefficient of Determination (R-squared):
Democrat = 0.774980
Republican = 0.019870

Democrat Popular Vote = .00709x - 13.667

;where "x" is the election year.

Year	1972	1980	1984	1988	1992	1996	2000	2004
Democrat	0.25	0.40	0.39	0.48	0.47	0.49	0.47	0.50
Prediction	0.31	0.36	0.39	0.42	0.45	0.48	0.51	0.53
Accuracy%	75.3	90.7	97.9	87.2	95.1	98.0	93.2	93.9

Source: Dave Leip's Atlas of U.S. Presidential Elections, uselectionatlas.org

Kentucky

Coefficient of Determination (R-squared):
Democrat = 0.727414
Republican = 0.328365

Democrat Popular Vote = .00834x - 15.995

;where "x" is the election year.

Year	1972	1980	1984	1988	1992	1996	2000	2004
Democrat	0.37	0.62	0.54	0.58	0.67	0.64	0.64	0.71
Prediction	0.45	0.52	0.55	0.58	0.62	0.65	0.68	0.72
Accuracy%	79.0	83.7	98.2	99.6	92.6	98.0	93.2	99.5

Source: Dave Leip's Atlas of U.S. Presidential Elections, uselectionatlas.org

Iowa

Coefficient of Determination (R-squared):
Democrat = 0.714176
Republican = 0.037103

Democrat Popular Vote = .00640x - 12.122

;where "x" is the election year.

Year	1972	1980	1984	1988	1992	1996	2000	2004
Democrat	0.50	0.51	0.61	0.67	0.59	0.62	0.64	0.74
Prediction	0.50	0.55	0.57	0.60	0.62	0.65	0.68	0.70
Accuracy%	99.9	92.3	94.7	89.3	93.5	95.2	94.2	94.5

Source: Dave Leip's Atlas of U.S. Presidential Elections, uselectionatlas.org

Louisiana

Coefficient of Determination (R-squared):
Democrat = 0.682426
Republican = 0.235176

Democrat Popular Vote = .01463x - 28.396

;where "x" is the election year.

Year	1972	1980	1984	1988	1992	1996	2000	2004
Democrat	0.30	0.71	0.65	0.72	0.82	0.93	0.79	0.82
Prediction	0.46	0.58	0.64	0.69	0.75	0.81	0.87	0.93
Accuracy%	45.6	81.5	97.6	96.8	92.3	87.5	90.2	86.8

Source: Dave Leip's Atlas of U.S. Presidential Elections, uselectionatlas.org

---

Alabama

Coefficient of Determination (R-squared):
Democrat = 0.660459
Republican = 0.567048

Democrat Popular Vote = .01127x - 21.822

;where "x" is the election year.

Year	1972	1980	1984	1988	1992	1996	2000	2004
Democrat	0.26	0.64	0.55	0.55	0.69	0.66	0.70	0.69
Prediction	0.39	0.49	0.53	0.58	0.62	0.67	0.71	0.76
Accuracy%	46.3	76.2	96.1	95.3	89.9	99.5	97.9	91.1

Source: Dave Leip's Atlas of U.S. Presidential Elections, uselectionatlas.org

Nebraska

Coefficient of Determination (R-squared):
Democrat = 0.659135
Republican = 0.061281

Democrat Popular Vote = .00278x - 5.3212

;where "x" is the election year.

Year	1972	1980	1984	1988	1992	1996	2000	2004
Democrat	0.17	0.17	0.19	0.26	0.22	0.24	0.23	0.25
Prediction	0.17	0.19	0.20	0.21	0.22	0.23	0.24	0.26
Accuracy%	98.2	86.7	93.4	81.4	97.6	98.7	94.4	99.4

Source: Dave Leip's Atlas of U.S. Presidential Elections, uselectionatlas.org

---

Massachusetts

Coefficient of Determination (R-squared):
Democrat = 0.659030
Republican = 0.220114

Democrat Popular Vote = .01803x - 34.461

;where "x" is the election year.

Year	1972	1980	1984	1988	1992	1996	2000	2004
Democrat	1.33	1.05	1.24	1.40	1.32	1.57	1.62	1.80
Prediction	1.10	1.25	1.32	1.39	1.46	1.53	1.61	1.68
Accuracy%	82.7	81.8	93.7	99.2	89.1	97.6	99.4	93.1

Source: Dave Leip's Atlas of U.S. Presidential Elections, uselectionatlas.org

Wyoming

Coefficient of Determination (R-squared):
Democrat = 0.650640
Republican = 0.297012

Democrat Popular Vote = .00088x - 1.6794

;where "x" is the election year.

Year	1972	1980	1984	1988	1992	1996	2000	2004
Democrat	0.04	0.05	0.05	0.07	0.07	0.08	0.06	0.07
Prediction	0.05	0.05	0.06	0.06	0.06	0.07	0.07	0.07
Accuracy%	96.0	92.5	93.9	89.6	93.4	86.2	83.2	95.3

Source: Dave Leip's Atlas of U.S. Presidential Elections, uselectionatlas.org

---

Arkansas

Coefficient of Determination (R-squared):
Democrat = 0.646258
Republican = 0.021646

Democrat Popular Vote = .00747x - 14.459

;where "x" is the election year.

Year	1972	1980	1984	1988	1992	1996	2000	2004
Democrat	0.20	0.40	0.34	0.35	0.51	0.48	0.42	0.47
Prediction	0.26	0.32	0.35	0.38	0.41	0.44	0.47	0.50
Accuracy%	67.2	81.4	95.5	90.2	81.7	93.3	88.1	93.0

Source: Dave Leip's Atlas of U.S. Presidential Elections, uselectionatlas.org

District of Columbia

Coefficient of Determination (R-squared):
Democrat = 0.586668
Republican = 0.675194

Democrat Popular Vote = .00195x - 3.7141

;where "x" is the election year.

Year	1972	1980	1984	1988	1992	1996	2000	2004
Democrat	0.13	0.13	0.18	0.16	0.19	0.16	0.17	0.20
Prediction	0.13	0.15	0.15	0.16	0.17	0.18	0.19	0.19
Accuracy%	97.1	87.2	85.8	98.1	88.4	87.4	91.9	95.4

Mississippi

Coefficient of Determination (R-squared):
Democrat = 0.549785
Republican = 0.231244

Democrat Popular Vote = .00711x - 13.773

;where "x" is the election year.

Year	1972	1980	1984	1988	1992	1996	2000	2004
Democrat	0.13	0.43	0.35	0.36	0.40	0.39	0.40	0.46
Prediction	0.24	0.30	0.33	0.36	0.38	0.41	0.44	0.47
Accuracy%	9.4	69.6	92.9	97.7	95.9	95.4	91.2	97.5

Source: Dave Leip's Atlas of U.S. Presidential Elections, uselectionatlas.org

Montana

Coefficient of Determination (R-squared):
Democrat = 0.498962
Republican = 0.157268

Democrat Popular Vote = .00144x - 2.7224

;where "x" is the election year.

Year	1972	1980	1984	1988	1992	1996	2000	2004
Democrat	0.12	0.12	0.15	0.17	0.15	0.17	0.14	0.17
Prediction	0.12	0.13	0.14	0.15	0.15	0.16	0.16	0.17
Accuracy%	97.5	85.9	95.7	86.6	98.4	94.0	80.7	97.5

Source: Dave Leip's Atlas of U.S. Presidential Elections, uselectionatlas.org

---

South Dakota

Coefficient of Determination (R-squared):
Democrat = 0.077824
Republican = 0.055647

Democrat Popular Vote = .00042x - .70985

;where "x" is the election year.

Year	1972	1980	1984	1988	1992	1996	2000	2004
Democrat	0.14	0.10	0.12	0.15	0.12	0.14	0.12	0.15
Prediction	0.12	0.13	0.13	0.13	0.13	0.13	0.13	0.14
Accuracy%	87.4	79.0	90.3	88.7	95.3	95.1	87.1	91.0

Source: Dave Leip's Atlas of U.S. Presidential Elections, uselectionatlas.org

North Dakota

Coefficient of Determination (R-squared):
Democrat = 0.072460
Republican = 0.036751

Democrat Popular Vote = .00035x - .59132

;where "x" is the election year.

Year	1972	1980	1984	1988	1992	1996	2000	2004
Democrat	0.10	0.08	0.10	0.13	0.10	0.11	0.10	0.11
Prediction	0.10	0.10	0.10	0.10	0.10	0.11	0.11	0.11
Accuracy%	96.5	74.1	96.8	80.3	95.2	98.5	88.0	97.3

Source: Dave Leip's Atlas of U.S. Presidential Elections, uselectionatlas.org

---

West Virginia

Coefficient of Determination (R-squared):
Democrat = 0.004266
Republican = 0.151916

Democrat Popular Vote = .00017x - .00789

;where "x" is the election year.

Year	1972	1980	1984	1988	1992	1996	2000	2004
Democrat	0.28	0.37	0.33	0.34	0.33	0.33	0.30	0.33
Prediction	0.32	0.32	0.32	0.32	0.32	0.33	0.33	0.33
Accuracy%	84.1	87.8	98.6	95.0	98.1	99.3	89.6	99.9

Source: Dave Leip's Atlas of U.S. Presidential Elections, uselectionatlas.org

States with Low Trend Correlation

A detailed review of the state statistics that posses a low Democrat Coefficient of Determination (or trend correlation) reveal that many have decreasing or relatively unchanging votes casts for the Democratic candidate. Consequently, the Democratic Trend Phenomenon may still exist in a particular state, but is masked due to a decrease in population. That is to say that the Democratic votes cast may be increasing while the population is decreasing, therefore canceling out the trend pattern. In essence, the decreasing or unchanging population may yield a lower Coefficient of Determination. To study this further, review Table 10-4 which present each state's population change from 1970 to 2000 in addition to the state's Democrat and Republican Coefficient of Determination.

Table 10-4 - State Population Change, 1970-2000
Sorted by State Population Change
(million)

NAME	DEM7204R2	REP7204R2	POP 1970	POP 2000	Chg %
Nevada	0.857366	0.726159	0.55	2.00	265.5
Arizona	0.952441	0.674109	2.01	5.13	155.4
Florida	0.954478	0.552972	7.52	15.98	112.5
Utah	0.832252	0.365817	1.13	2.23	96.8
Alaska	0.901508	0.772220	0.33	0.63	92.0
Colorado	0.900601	0.454449	2.40	4.30	78.9
Texas	0.901074	0.536691	11.76	20.85	77.3
Washington	0.954439	0.317352	3.45	5.89	71.0
Georgia	0.846576	0.656186	4.81	8.19	70.3
Idaho	0.828829	0.419631	0.76	1.29	69.5
New Mexico	0.937213	0.239209	1.08	1.82	68.8
California	0.890154	0.000154	20.58	33.87	64.5
New Hampshire	0.879800	0.237078	0.78	1.24	58.1
Oregon	0.888834	0.385464	2.20	3.42	55.9
North Carolina	0.930283	0.629555	5.30	8.05	52.0
South Carolina	0.881333	0.702156	2.72	4.01	47.6
Virginia	0.972371	0.602409	4.83	7.08	46.6

Table 10-4 - State Population Change, 1970-2000
Sorted by State Population Change
(million)

NAME	DEM7204R2	REP7204R2	POP 1970	POP 2000	Chg %
Hawaii	0.940587	0.002314	0.83	1.21	46.4
Wyoming	0.650640	0.297184	0.35	0.49	42.4
Tennessee	0.831106	0.505209	4.09	5.69	39.2
Delaware	0.833096	0.690983	0.57	0.78	36.6
Arkansas	0.646258	0.021653	2.02	2.67	32.5
Vermont	0.958905	0.007157	0.46	0.61	31.4
Oklahoma	0.774980	0.019872	2.66	3.45	29.8
Maryland	0.955097	0.076671	4.08	5.30	29.8
Minnesota	0.820806	0.219966	3.87	4.92	27.2
Alabama	0.660459	0.567065	3.54	4.45	25.6
Montana	0.498962	0.157166	0.72	0.90	25.5
Mississippi	0.549785	0.231232	2.31	2.84	23.3
Maine	0.931444	0.012105	1.03	1.27	23.2
Kentucky	0.727414	0.328352	3.34	4.04	21.2
Wisconsin	0.804928	0.184295	4.50	5.36	19.2
Kansas	0.787273	0.043813	2.26	2.69	19.2
Louisiana	0.682426	0.235197	3.76	4.47	18.8
Missouri	0.895820	0.024115	4.75	5.60	17.7
Indiana	0.847972	0.035012	5.30	6.08	14.8
New Jersey	0.933042	0.303119	7.34	8.41	14.7
Nebraska	0.659135	0.061283	1.52	1.71	12.7
South Dakota	0.077824	0.055617	0.68	0.75	11.4
Connecticut	0.900589	0.359908	3.07	3.41	10.9
Illinois	0.897718	0.379359	11.26	12.42	10.3
Massachusetts	0.659030	0.220121	5.76	6.35	10.2
Michigan	0.866897	0.000170	9.02	9.94	10.1
Rhode Island	0.861474	0.406165	0.98	1.05	7.4
Ohio	0.858777	0.001273	10.75	11.35	5.6
New York	0.881509	0.505964	18.35	18.98	3.4

Table 10-4 - State Population Change, 1970-2000
Sorted by State Population Change
(million)

NAME	DEM7204R2	REP7204R2	POP 1970	POP 2000	Chg %
Pennsylvania	0.813496	0.045050	11.90	12.28	3.2
Iowa	0.714176	0.037104	2.86	2.93	2.3
North Dakota	0.072460	0.036809	0.63	0.64	1.8
West Virginia	0.004266	0.151903	1.80	1.81	0.6
District of Columbia	0.586602	0.020216	0.74	0.57	-23.1

Source: U.S. Census Bureau, Demographic Trends in the 20th Century, 2002 (Table #1)

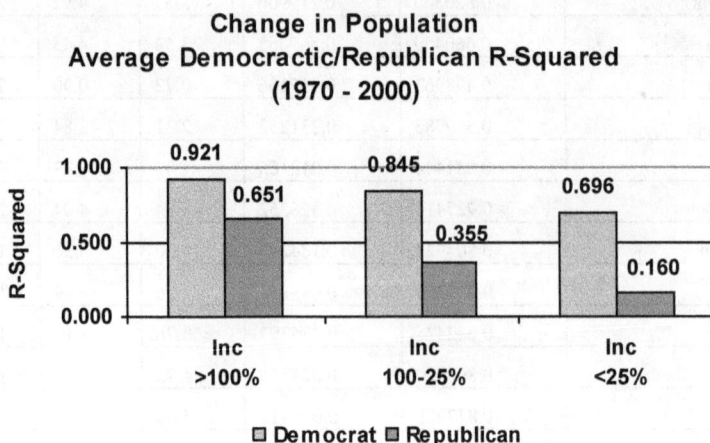

Change in Population
Average Democractic/Republican R-Squared
(1970 - 2000)

□ Democrat ▨ Republican

Figure 10-3 - Change in Population, Average Democrat/Republican R-Squared
(1970 - 2000)

At first glance, Table 10-4 may not readily reveal that the states with the lowest population change also have the lowest Coefficient of Determination.[82] However, if the states are grouped together by their increase in population, the effect on the Coefficient of Determination

[82] The national population increased from 203.2 million in 1970 to 281.4 million in 2000 with an increase of 38.5% (Source: U.S. Census Bureau, Decennial Census Population, 1900 to 2000)

comes to light. For instance, Figure 10-3 shows a graph with the states grouped into three ranges of population increase: 1) less than 25%; 2) 25% to 100%; and 3) greater than 100%. As Figure 10-3 indicates, those states that have a population increase from, 1970 to 2000, which is less than 25% have an average Democrat Coefficient of Determination of .696. The corresponding average Republican Coefficient of Determination is calculated to be .160. However, the states with a population increase of 25% to 100% have an average Democrat Coefficient of Determination of .845 with Republican Coefficient of Determination of .355. The states with the highest population increase, which is greater than 100%, have a Democrat and Republican Coefficient of Determination of .921 and .651 respectively. In each case the decreasing population change yields a decrease in the Coefficient of Determination.

Chapter 11

Mapping the Trend

"A picture is worth a thousand words."

Napoleon Bonaparte

Introduction

Additional analysis of the Democratic Trend can be achieved using "thematic maps." As Napoleon Bonaparte stated, *"A picture is worth a thousand words."* Thematic maps display spatial data using specific themes. For example, each state can be presented on a map with different shading depending upon its Democratic Trend's Coefficient of Determination. The next several pages present a series of maps that compare the population increase with the states' Coefficient of Determination.

Map Analysis

As discussed in Chapter 10, the states with the lowest population increase also tend to have the lowest Coefficient of Determination. Comparing the states population change map (Figure 11-1) to the next two maps (Figure 11-2 and 11-3) further validates the conclusions of Chapter 10. Further analysis shows a dramatic difference between the Republican Trend maps and the Republican baseline maps. Very few states show even a moderate Coefficient of Determination on the Republican Trend maps while a sizable amount of states show high Coefficient of Determination on the Republican baseline maps. Finally, the Other candidates' upper limit maps (Figure 11-6) indicate a lower Coefficient of Determination in the southern states. This is in direct contrast with the high change in population in those states. Most likely this was caused be the steady transition of Other candidates' voters (old democrats) switching their votes to Republican candidates.

Population Change

Figure 11-1 displays a map that depicts the states population change from 1970 to 2000. The states with a population increase of less than 25% have no shading. The states with 25% to 100% population increase are displayed in a light gray shade. Those states with greater than 100% are displayed in a darker gray shade.

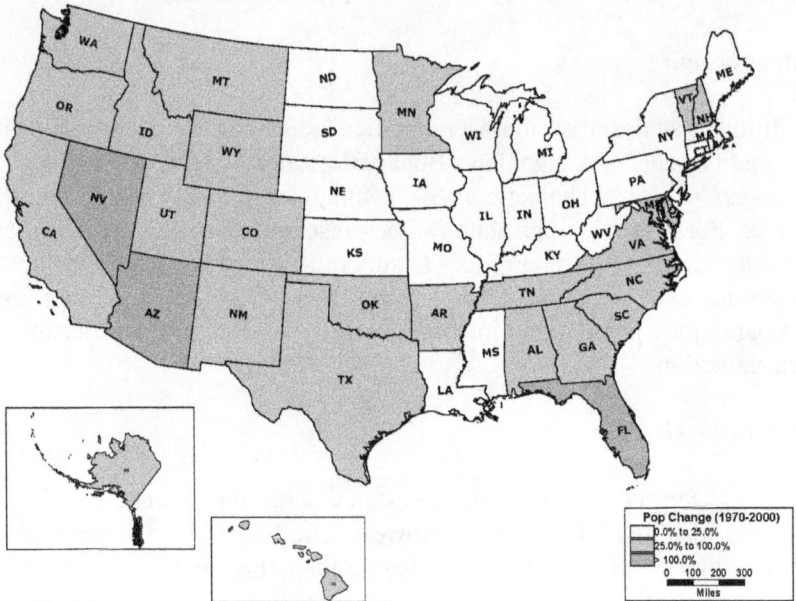

Figure 11-1 - Population Change (1970 - 2000)

Democratic Trend (1972-2004)

Figure 11-2 displays a map that depicts the Coefficient of Determination (r^2) of the popular vote for the Democratic candidate for president from 1972 to 2004 (excluding 1976). The states with a Coefficient of Determination of less than .80 have no shading. The states with a Coefficient of Determination between .80 to .90 are displayed in a light gray shade. Those states with greater than .90 are displayed in a darker gray shade.

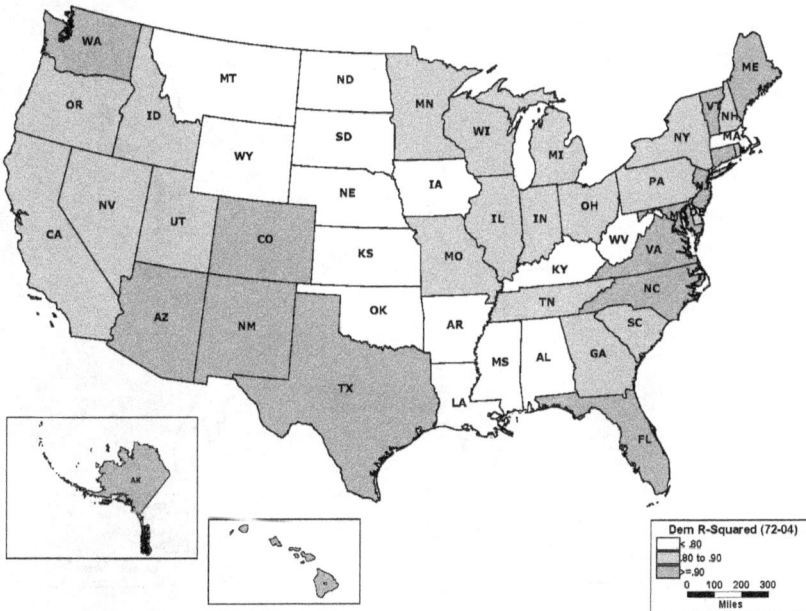

Figure 11-2 - Democrat Coefficient of Determination
(1972 - 2004)

Republican Trend (1972-2004)

Figure 11-3 displays a map that depicts the Coefficient of Determination
(r^2) of the popular vote for the Republican candidate for president from
1972 to 2004 (excluding 1976). The states with a Coefficient of
Determination of less than .60 have no shading. The states with a
Coefficient of Determination between .60 to .70 are displayed in a light
gray shade. Those states with greater than .70 are displayed in a darker
gray shade.

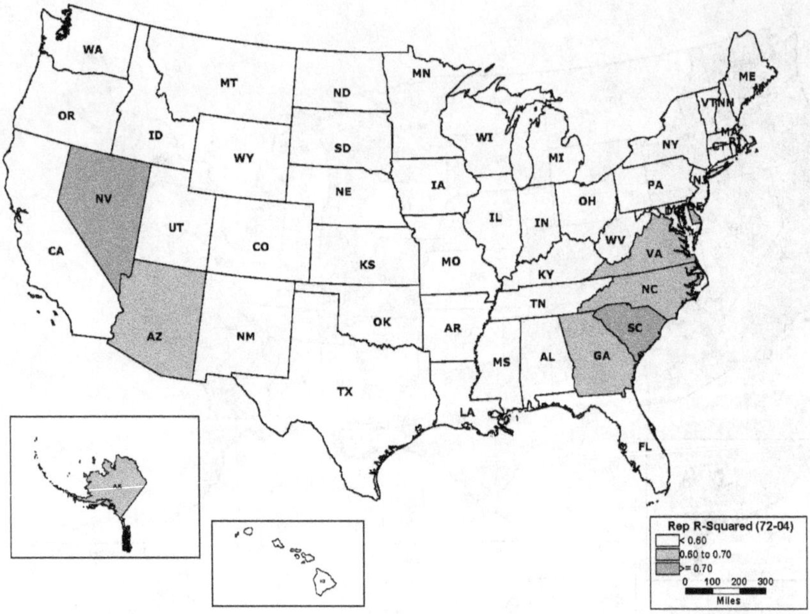

Figure 11-3 - Republican Coefficient of Determination
(1972 - 2004)

Democrat Baseline Trend (1948, 1968 & 1992)

Figure 11-4 displays a map that depicts the Coefficient of Determination (r^2) of the popular vote for the Democratic candidate for president for the 1948, 1968, and 1992 elections. The states with a Coefficient of Determination of less than .80 have no shading. The states with a Coefficient of Determination between .80 to .90 are displayed in a light gray shade. Those states with greater than .90 are displayed in a darker gray shade.

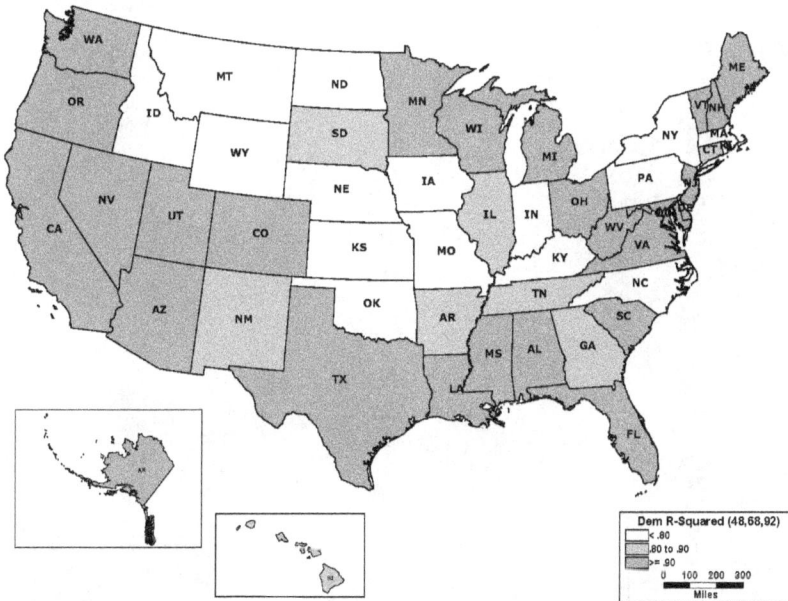

Figure 11-4 - Democrat Baseline Coefficient of Determination
(1948, 1968 & 1992)

Republican Baseline Trend (1948, 1968 & 1992)

Figure 11-5 displays a map that depicts the Coefficient of Determination
(r^2) of the popular vote for the Republican candidate for president for the
1948, 1968, and 1992 elections. The states with a Coefficient of
Determination of less than .80 have no shading. The states with a
Coefficient of Determination between .80 to .90 are displayed in a light
gray shade. Those states with greater than .90 are displayed in a darker
gray shade.[83]

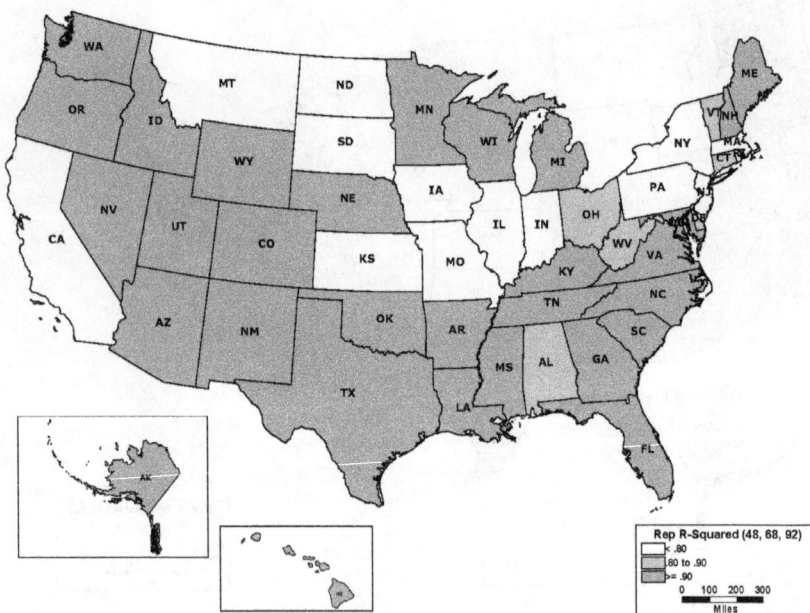

Figure 11-5 - Republican Baseline Coefficient of Determination
(1948, 1968 & 1992)

---

[83] Notice the large amount of states with a high Coefficient of Determination.

Other Upper Limit Trend (1948, 1968 & 1992)

Figure 11-6 displays a map that depicts the Coefficient of Determination (r^2) of the popular vote for the Other candidates for president for the 1948, 1968, and 1992 elections. The states with a Coefficient of Determination of less than .80 have no shading. The states with between .80 to .90 Coefficient of Determination are displayed in a light gray shade. Those states with greater than .90 are displayed in a darker gray shade.[84]

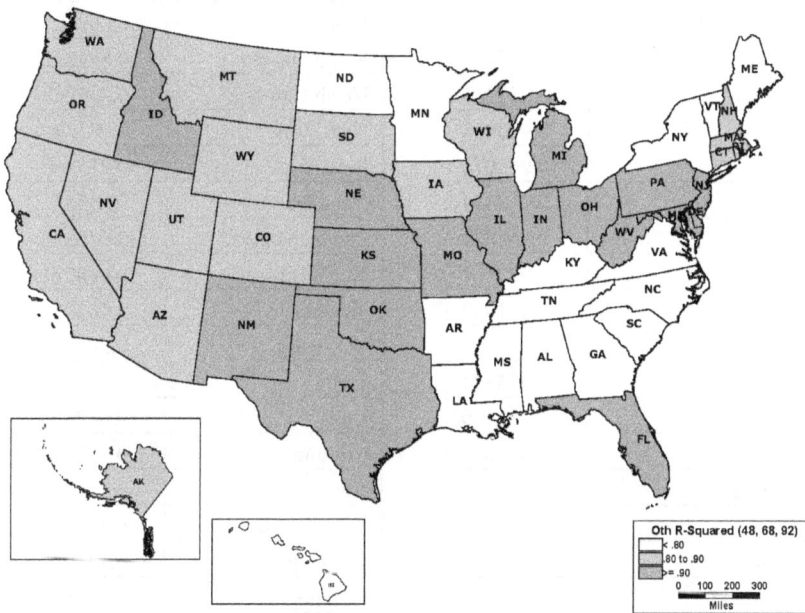

Figure 11-6 - Other Candidates Upper Limit Coefficient of Determination (1948, 1968 & 1992)

---

[84] Notice the unshaded states in the south. After the fracturing of the electorate in 1968, there was a steady transition of Other candidate voters (old democrats) becoming Republicans.

Table 11-1 - State Coefficient of Determination for Democratic
Candidates for President
(1948, 1968, 1992)

State	r^2	State	r^2
Ohio	0.999487	Arizona	0.904549
California	0.997591	New Mexico	0.898332
Minnesota	0.996633	Connecticut	0.882227
South Carolina	0.989558	Tennessee	0.876120
Delaware	0.989119	Georgia	0.865729
Maryland	0.987747	Arkansas	0.861266
West Virginia	0.984706	Illinois	0.860857
Mississippi	0.984100	South Dakota	0.834221
Oregon	0.971735	North Carolina	0.799069
Texas	0.970865	New York	0.781749
Virginia	0.965014	Indiana	0.773967
Alabama	0.963614	Montana	0.695571
Vermont	0.961821	Pennsylvania	0.670368
Washington	0.957635	North Dakota	0.618021
Wisconsin	0.951932	Kentucky	0.562040
Louisiana	0.950626	Wyoming	0.503054
New Hampshire	0.935324	Idaho	0.429378
Michigan	0.935159	Iowa	0.387475
New Jersey	0.933831	Missouri	0.318283
Florida	0.933701	Kansas	0.236214
Utah	0.933412	Massachusetts	0.230465
Maine	0.926102	Rhode Island	0.140990
Colorado	0.915685	Oklahoma	0.025669
Nevada	0.914737	Nebraska	0.004250

Note: Alaska, Hawaii, and Washington D.C were not included in the analysis.

Table 11-2 - State Coefficient of Determination for Republican
Candidates for President
(1948, 1968,1992)

State	r^2	State	r^2
Kentucky	0.999345	Oregon	0.931186
South Carolina	0.999140	Nebraska	0.918426
Virginia	0.998687	Mississippi	0.907394
Arkansas	0.998653	Wyoming	0.903115
Tennessee	0.998297	Vermont	0.898287
Texas	0.998225	Alabama	0.886810
North Carolina	0.998153	Ohio	0.879281
New Hampshire	0.997498	West Virginia	0.872990
Colorado	0.993068	Delaware	0.836438
Arizona	0.992881	Connecticut	0.823701
Maryland	0.989668	Montana	0.792945
Florida	0.985534	California	0.777465
Oklahoma	0.985466	New Jersey	0.769335
Maine	0.982540	Missouri	0.699135
Utah	0.980005	North Dakota	0.616111
Georgia	0.979901	New York	0.568919
Washington	0.976841	Massachusetts	0.447364
Nevada	0.969347	Indiana	0.393475
Louisiana	0.961538	Illinois	0.312679
Idaho	0.959099	Kansas	0.191006
Michigan	0.953645	Pennsylvania	0.171573
Wisconsin	0.953033	South Dakota	0.087522
Minnesota	0.944170	Rhode Island	0.064239
New Mexico	0.937797	Iowa	0.000681

Note: Alaska, Hawaii, and Washington D.C were not included in the analysis.

Table 11-3 - State Coefficient of Determination for
Other Candidates for President
(1948, 1968,1992)

State	r^2	State	r^2
Illinois	0.999646	Nevada	0.884795
Delaware	0.999612	Montana	0.878576
New Jersey	0.999552	Arizona	0.877285
Ohio	0.998153	Rhode Island	0.876697
Indiana	0.996535	Washington	0.868312
Missouri	0.993229	Utah	0.864466
Pennsylvania	0.991387	Oregon	0.857641
Texas	0.990157	Massachusetts	0.850235
Florida	0.989820	New Hampshire	0.847498
Michigan	0.986085	North Dakota	0.845059
Oklahoma	0.975145	Minnesota	0.840039
Maryland	0.973338	Vermont	0.836663
New Mexico	0.960623	Maine	0.806260
West Virginia	0.952786	Virginia	0.802551
Kansas	0.950604	Kentucky	0.762494
Nebraska	0.949702	New York	0.614571
Idaho	0.935679	North Carolina	0.397039
Iowa	0.927199	Georgia	0.217214
Wyoming	0.920231	South Carolina	0.106657
Wisconsin	0.912041	Tennessee	0.104457
Connecticut	0.903618	Arkansas	0.080174
Colorado	0.898928	Mississippi	0.073184
California	0.894097	Louisiana	0.001721
South Dakota	0.892040	Alabama	0.000395

Note: Alaska, Hawaii, and Washington D.C were not included in the analysis.

PART 4

The Future Trend

Chapter 12

A New Electorate?

"Nothing lasts forever - not even your troubles."

Arnold H. Glasgow

Introduction

Excluding the 1976 election, the Democratic candidates' popular vote has increased in a consistent pattern for three decades or more. As stated before, this is an amazing phenomenon when considering: different candidates from all Parties; different current issues; varying voter turnout percentages and more. Nonetheless, through all of these differing conditions and circumstances, the Democratic popular vote for president continued to increase in a predictable fashion.

However, will this Trend change? And, can this Trend be altered? As Arnold H. Glasgow states, *"Nothing last forever - not even your troubles."* The answer to these questions may lie with the election of 2004. This chapter discusses a potential new trend for the Democratic candidate for president.

The 2004 Election

Most will agree that the 2004 campaign was filled with great debate and some may say controversy. Did this controversy and polarization cause the Democratic Trend to change? Maybe so. It seems that the popular vote for the Democratic candidate in 2004 deviated from the Democratic Trend line more than any other election since 1972, excluding 1976. This deviation from the estimate trend line can be seen in Figure 12-1.

Using the prediction techniques outlined in Chapter 8, the projected popular vote for 2004 should have been close to 54 million (see Table 12-1). However, the actual popular vote ended up being 59 million. The 2004 prediction underestimated the popular vote by over 5 million votes.

**Democratic Popular Vote
(1972 to 2004)**

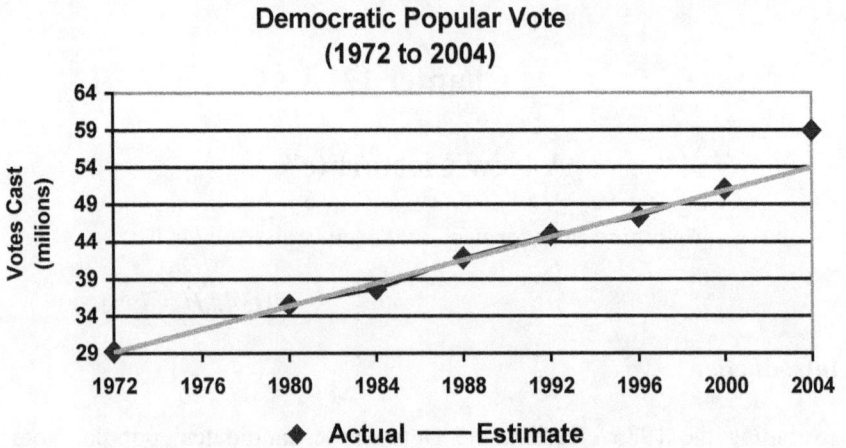

◆ **Actual** —— **Estimate**

Source: Dave Leip's Atlas of U.S. Presidential Elections, uselectionatlas.org

Figure 12-1 - Democrat Popular Vote (1972 - 2004)

Table 12-1 - Popular Vote for the Democratic Candidate and the Predicted
Amount (2004)
(millions)

	2004
Actual Popular Vote	59.0
Prediction Line ('72-'00)	54.0
%Accuracy	91.5%

Although the prediction remains reasonably precise and continues to validate the Democratic Trend, the deviation is notable.

In fact, as outlined in Chapter 8, the accuracy of the prediction for the 2004 election is 91.5% (see Table 12-1). The previous possible predicted values from 1988 to 2000 had an accuracy that ranged from 97.4% to roughly 99.5% (see Figure 12-2).

Predictions of the Popular Vote for the
Democractic Candidate
(1988 - 2004)

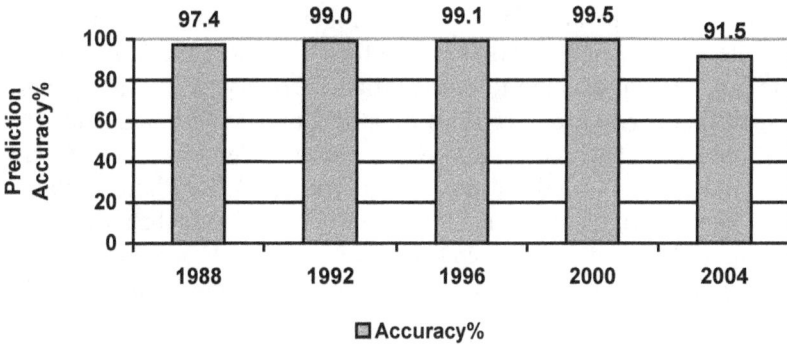

Figure 12-2- Accuracy of Regression Predictions
(1988 - 2004)

Why was the predicted value and accuracy so lower than the others? Or better stated, why was the actual popular vote so high? There are four probable answers:

Possibility One - Increase in Voting Age Population

My first thought was that there might have been an extraordinary increase in population from 2000 to 2004. In fact, according to the U.S. Census Bureau there was an increase in the voting age population of over 13 million persons from 2000 to 2004. However, from 1984 through 2000 the largest increase from election to election was 8.9 million. This dramatic increase from the prior years led me to believe that the increase in Kerry's vote was tied to the increase in voting age population from 2000 to 2004.

Nonetheless, from 1968 to 1984 the largest increase from election to election was over 19 million. At the same time there was not any major fluctuation of the vote for the Democratic candidate since 1968 excluding 2004 and of course 1976. Although I felt that the dramatic increase in the recent voting age population from 2000 to 2004 had something to do with the increase in Kerry's vote, it would be insignificant unless a sizable percentage registered and voted for John Kerry.

Possibility Two - New Democrat Voters

Similar to the first reason the second factor centered on the reality that organizations throughout the country had registered substantial amounts of voters in preparation for the November 2004 election. In fact, the increase in registered voters from 2000 to 2004 was the largest increase from presidential election to presidential election year in thirty years. To be specific, there were over 12 million new registered voters added from 2000 to 2004. The previous two presidential election cycles (1992 to 1996 and 1996 to 2000) added 1.1 million and 1.8 million respectively (see Chapter 12). Clearly, the 2000 to 2004 cycle was substantially larger than the increase of any in recent years. However, these newly registered voters could not add to John Kerry's votes unless they actually voted.

One of the distinctive aspects of the 2004 campaign was the extraordinary amount of effort placed into voter registration efforts. According to the U.S. Census Bureau's Current Population Survey, the previous two presidential election cycles (1992 to 1996 and 1996 to 2000) added 1.1 million and 1.8 million respectively. This is minute compared to the estimated increase for 2000 to 2004. Most analysis show that the 2004 election cycle included almost record breaking voter registration numbers. For instance, according to the U.S. Census Bureau's report on Voting & Registration for the November 2004 Election, there were approximately 142.1 million registered voters at the time of the election.

Table 12-2 - Overall U.S. Registration, 1972-2004
(millions)

Year	Registered	%	Increase
2004	142.1	65.9	12.6
2000	129.5	63.9	1.8
1996	127.7	65.9	1.1
1992	126.6	68.2	8.0
1988	118.6	66.6	2.5
1984	116.1	68.3	11.1
1980	105.0	66.9	7.3
1976	97.7	66.7	-.7[85]
1972	98.5	72.3	11.9

Note: The values have been rounded to the nearest single decimal point.

Source: U.S. Census Bureau Current Population Survey, 2000 & Voting & Registration in the November 2004 Election Online Tables

---

[85] There was a decrease in the number of registered voters from 1972 to 1976.

This equates to an increase of 12.6 million voters from 2000.[86] Thus, this increase would be the largest rise in registered voters in more than thirty years (see Table 12-2). However, these newly registered voters could not add to Kerry's popular vote unless they actually voted and voted for him.

In 2004, exit polls from CNN revealed that 11% of the voters were first time voters. In 1996 and 2000 exit polls by CNN revealed that only 9% of the voters were first time voter. My conclusion was that the dramatic increase in new registered voters most likely influenced the number of first time voters.

% of Votes Cast Who Were First Time Voters
1996, 2000, 2004

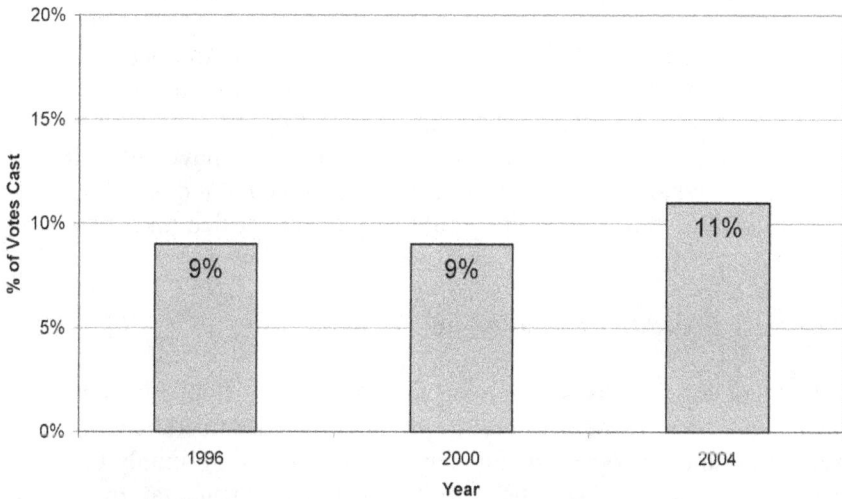

Source: CNN.com Exit Polls 1996, 2000, 2004

Figure 12-3 - % of Votes Cast Who Were First Time Voters

This increase of 2% of first time voters (11% minus 9%) resulted in an additional 2.4 million new voters. The same exit polls indicated that

---

[86] Using CNN's exit poll data finds that 11% of the 2004 presidential voters were new voters. With approximately 122 million votes cast, this equates to approximately 13.4 million newly registered voters.

Kerry received 53% of these voters. This equates to 1.3 million voters more than if the percentage of first time voters equated to 9% (the 1996 or 2000 levels). The additional of 1.3 million voters for Kerry did not completely answer the increase of the trend. There must have been another factor involved.

Possibility Three - Partisan Switch

The third possible contributor to the increase in the popular vote for the Democratic candidate, John Kerry, is analogous to the circumstances during the election of 1976. That is to say that events occurring prior to the election may have induced a small realignment in the electorate. The evidence was that this unknown issue did not change the electorate as much as Watergate, but it may have altered it nonetheless. There was only one issue in 2004 that became extremely dominant, "the Iraq war."

In March of 2003, a Gallup poll reveal that 75% of Americans felt the U.S. did "not" make a mistake in sending troops to Iraq. By 2004, a Gallup poll showed a fairly dramatic decrease to 48%. It could be that the dramatic growing opposition to the war might have influenced a portion of the Non-Democrat electorate to switch over and vote for Kerry. Unfortunately, this possibility could not be quantified like the other options.

The Answer to Altering the Trend

I felt that the jury is still out on whether the portion of voters who switched or even those that were newly registered Democratic voters will act as the same as consistent core base voters. They may simply be a new connection that bridges the gap between the Democrat and Non-Democrat electorate or even voters who choose to not vote. On the other hand, the 2004 election could be the beginning of another electoral alignment.

Most likely, the combination of an exceptionally high increase in voting age population and registered voters, in addition to a partial switching of Non-Democrats, yielded a slight divergence from the normal trend. In other words, the extraordinary confluence of forces placed on the election at the same time expanded the Democrat electorate and altered the popular vote from the normal trend.

Regardless of the reason, this notable deviation brings to light the answer to the question, "will this Trend change?" The answer seems to be "yes" - at least when it comes to unique circumstances. However, two issues remain: 1) will the influx of new and possibly disproportionate registered voters change the stability of the Democratic Trend?; and 2) have the Democrat and Non-Democrat electorates begun to merge back into one? Unfortunately, these questions may not be fully answered until after future elections. Nonetheless, the next chapter delves into the possible outcome for the 2008 election and beyond.

Chapter 13

Predicting 2008 and Beyond

"Change is coming to America."

Barack Obama

Introduction

Undoubtedly, the question lingering in most people's minds after reading through the other chapters in this book is, "what will be the popular vote for the Democratic candidate in 2008 and beyond?" It stands to reason that we should be able to predict, with a fair degree of accuracy, the popular vote for the 2008 election and maybe beyond. However, as Barack Obama states, *"Change is coming to America."* Therefore, without sounding as if I am avoiding the challenge, we may not know which direction our electorate may take. This is due to the potential development of a new group of core Democratic voters or new "cross-over" group of voters from the Non-Democrat electorate to the Democrat Electorate. Be that as it may, let us first use the existing trend formula to calculate the 2008 election.

Predicting 2008 Using the Existing Trend (1972 to 2004)

Calculating using the 1972 to 2004 trend line equation[87] and substituting the election of 2008, the popular vote is predicted to be approximately 59.4 million votes. Since this amounts to the same popular vote that Senator John Kerry received in 2004, this projected amount is most definitely inaccurate. Thus, a new calculation should be determined for the popular vote and include the voting increase in the 2004 election.

---

[87] The regression equation using the election years from 1972 to 2004 would be: Votes Cast $= 0.8707x - 1689$; where x is the election year.

Predicting 2008 Considering the Increase in 2004

As noted previously, the popular vote for John Kerry, in 2004, was relatively higher than the predicted values (see Chapter 8, Table 8-5). The amount of votes cast exceeded the predicted value by over 5 million votes. Clearly the influx of new Democratic voters (at least for one election) altered the trend line. Since, the 2004 election was the only election that lied noticeably outside of the trend line, the determination was made to "not" develop a new trend line.[88] Instead the additional 5 million voters in 2004 were simply added to the prediction.

As a result, if the votes cast for the Democratic candidate in 2008 turns out to be close to 59 million, an assumption can be made that the old trend remains intact, the election of 2004 was a small anomaly, and the electorate has not been altered. However, if the Democratic candidate, Senator Barack Obama, receives greater than or close to 64 million votes, a different assumption may well be made. That is to say that the Trend has been altered, and there's been a change in our electorate.

An expanded view of the increase may assume that there could be an additional 5 million voters added to the 2008 election similar to the 2004 election. Assuming this possibility, Barack Obama would receive an estimated 69 million votes.

The Future Direction

It is uncertain which path the popular vote for the Democratic candidate will take. The popular vote may move along the path of the existing Trend or move along a new Trend as in 2004 election.

If the votes cast for Democratic and Non-Democratic candidates are plotted on a graph it reveals two distinct trend lines. As figure 13-1 indicates, the popular vote for the Democratic candidates is increasing at a faster rate than the popular vote for the Non-Democratic candidates.

---

[88] Since 2004 is the only election that has deviated, a new trend line may be developed after obtaining the results of the 2008 election. The 2000, 2004, and 2008 elections can be used to define the new trend. Furthermore, it is possible that because of certain factors, possibly due to demographic changes; the trend may have been altered from a linear trend to an exponential trend.

To illustrate the dramatic differences between the trend lines, simply compare the increase of the Non-Democratic and Democratic popular vote from 1972 to 2004. The Non-Democratic popular vote increased 10 million from 1972 to 2004. Conversely, the Democratic popular vote increased almost three times as much as the Non-Democratic or 30 million during the same period of time.

Democratic/Non-Democrat Candidates
Votes Cast w/Trend Lines
(1972 to 2004 w/o 1976)

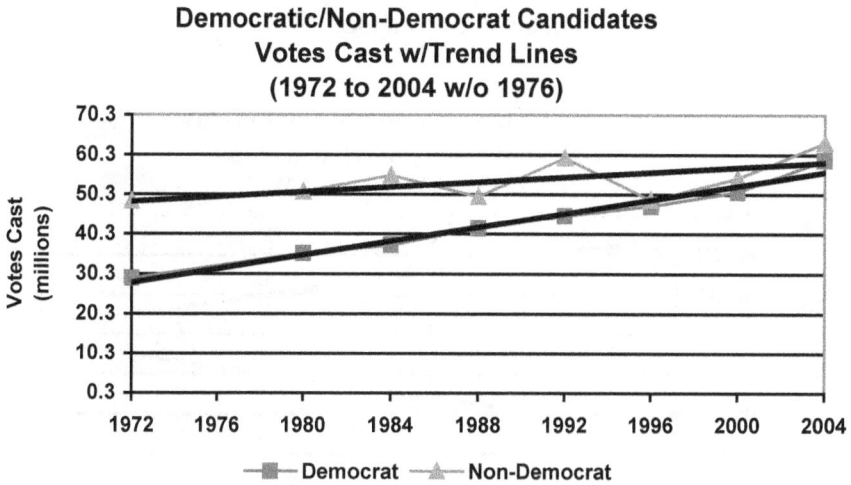

Source: Dave Leip's Atlas of U.S. Presidential Elections, uselectionatlas.org

Figure 13-1 - Democratic/Non-Democrat Candidates Votes Cast (1972-2004)

As the Figure 13-1 graph displays, the trend lines appear as though they will eventually cross each other. Furthermore, it seems as though that crossing will occur in the near future. In fact, amazingly the formulas associated with "each" of the trend lines predict that there will be 59.4 million votes cast in the 2008 election.[89]

Given the results of the popular vote in the 2004 election, 59.4 million is most likely a very low projection. Furthermore, the accuracy of the Non-Democratic popular vote is too low[90] to rely on its projected value. However, the sharp increase of the popular vote for the Democratic

---

[89] The formula for the Non-Democratic candidates is: Votes Cast = 0.30426x − 551.49 - where x is the election year.
[90] The Coefficient of Determination for the Non-Democratic was a pitiful .3700.

candidates versus the Non-Democratic candidates is startling and should be eye opening for future Democratic and Republican candidates.

Nevertheless, a more interesting result is obtained when analyzing the "percentage" of the total popular vote for the Democratic and the Non-Democratic candidates. Again, from 1972 to 2004 the "percentage" trend line for the Democratic candidates steadily increases while the Non-Democrat candidates steadily decreases (see Figure 13-2).

Democratic/Non-Democrat Candidates
% of Votes Cast w/Trend Lines
(1972 to 2004 w/o 1976)

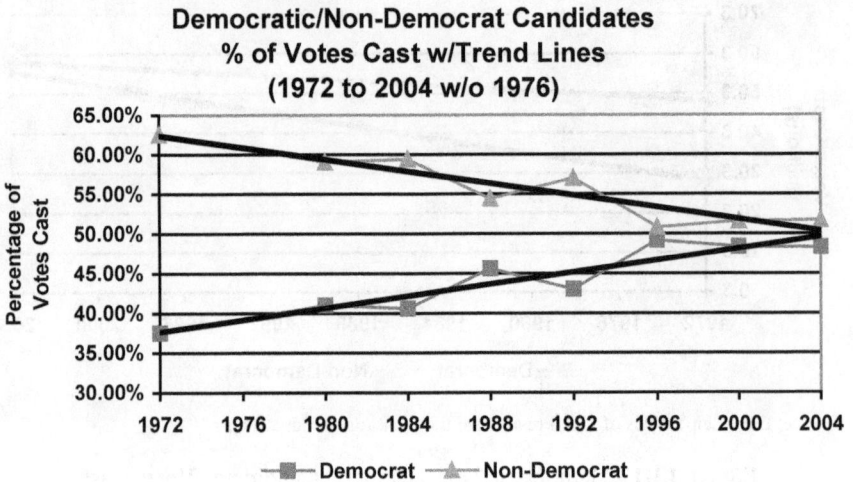

Source: Dave Leip's Atlas of U.S. Presidential Elections, uselectionatlas.org

Figure 13-2 - Democratic/Non-Democrat Candidates % of Votes Cast (1972-2004)

As with the popular vote, the increasing and decreasing slope of each trend is important since it indicates that eventually the two trends will cross paths. It is important to note that the percentage obtained by the candidates do not include those voters who "do not turnout." **Both of these trend lines can be altered if the nonvoters are motivated to turnout.** Nonetheless, this time the Non-Democratic and the Democratic Trend lines are mirror images of each other.[91] More importantly, the accuracy of the percentage trend lines from 1972 to 2004 is greater than

---

[91] The calculated Coefficient of Determination for the Democratic candidates remains at a respectable level of .8479.

or equal to 94.7% (the Non-Democratic Trend line is actually 94.9% accurate).[92]

Similar to the popular vote totals, the percentages reveal that the first election, directly after the overlap of the trend lines, should occur in 2008. In 2008, the estimated percentage of the votes cast for the combined Non-Democratic candidates is calculated to be **48.9%** (±2.5%). Considering the accuracy of 94.9%, Senator John McCain *plus the other Non-Majority Party candidates combined* should obtain somewhere between 46.4% to as much as 51.4% of the vote in 2008. On the other hand, the Democratic candidate's estimate is determined to be **51.1%** (±2.7%). Once again, taking in account the range in accuracy (94.7%), Senator Barack Obama should garner between 48.4% to 53.8% of the popular vote in 2008. If a reasonable estimate of at least 2% was anticipated for the Non-Majority Party candidates combined, Senator John McCain would be projected to receive 46.9%, with Senator Barack Obama receiving 51.1% (with an error for McCain as much as ± 2.5% and Obama as much as ± 2.7%). Given the margin of 4.2%, Barack Obama stands an excellent chance of becoming the winner of the popular vote.

There is a final note on the future. If the electorates continues to follow either one of the predicted trend lines, eventually, neither Republican nor Other candidates will be capable of garnering enough votes to win the popular vote.[93] At that time, the Democrat electorate will ultimately become larger than the Non-Democrat electorate. As a matter of fact, the Democratic candidate is projected to receive 52.6%, 54.1%, and 55.6% of the popular vote over the next three elections (2012, 2016, and 2020). This means that the Democratic candidate should win and continue to win the popular vote unless another major *realignment* of the electorate occurs. In other words, if our electorate remains fractured and the Democratic Trend Phenomenon continues to exist at the 1972 trajectory or greater level, future Democratic candidates should enjoy popular vote success and most likely the U.S. presidency for many years to come.

---

[92] The formula for the Democratic candidates is Votes Cast = 0.00373x − 6.97753 while the Non-Democratic candidate is Votes Cast = 0.00373x + 7.97753.

[93] Since the presidential winner requires the majority of electoral votes, the popular vote does not guarantee winning the presidency.

APPENDICES

Appendix A:
Statistical Equations

Note: The results that you obtain may vary slightly depending upon how many decimal places that you use in your calculations.

The regression equation utilized in this book uses the following simple line formula:

$$\hat{y} = bx + a$$

Where $\hat{y}$ is the predicted total popular vote for the Democratic candidate for a specific election year, x is the specific election year, b is the slope of the line, and a is the constant, (or y-intercept). The method used to calculate the regression equation is the "Least Squares" estimate. The basic formulas to calculate b and a are:

$$b = \frac{SP}{SS_x}$$

and

$$a = \frac{\sum Y}{n} - b\frac{\sum X}{n}$$

where

$$SP = \sum XY - \frac{\sum X \sum Y}{n}$$

and

$$SS_x = \sum X^2 - \frac{(\sum X)^2}{n}$$

The variable *n* is the number of election years analyzed, X represents the presidential elections years, and Y represents the popular vote for the Democratic candidate.

Next, to derive the correlation coefficient, *r*, (the Pearson correlation coefficient), the following formula is used:

$$r = \frac{SP}{\sqrt{SS_x SS_y}}$$

where SP and SSx have been defined above and SSy is calculated using:

$$SS_y = \sum Y^2 - \frac{\left(\sum Y\right)^2}{n}$$

The coefficient of Determination r^2 is calculated by squaring *r* or by using the following formula:

$$r^2 = \frac{SP^2}{SS_x SS_y}$$

Example:

Below provides an example of using the calculations to determine the regression equation for the elections 1980 through 2004:

The X's are the elections years of:

1980, 1984, 1988, 1992, 1996, 2000, 2004

Therefore, the n is 7 for seven years.

Appendix A: Statistical Equations

The Y's are the popular vote for the Democratic candidate:

35.480, 37.577, 41.809, 44.910, 47.400, 51.004, 59.028

Thus,

1. The slope b is calculated to be 0.920137

2. The y-intercept a is calculated to be -1787.6

Therefore, the regression line is determined to be:

$$y = .920137x - 1787.6$$

; where y is the predicted popular vote for the Democratic candidate; and x is the election year.

The correlation coefficient, r, is derived from:

$$r = \frac{412.221}{\sqrt{448 * 393.615}}$$

and

The coefficient of determination, r^2, is derived from:

$$r^2 = \frac{412.221^2}{448 * 393.615}$$

Thus,

1. The r is calculated to be 0.98165

2. The r^2 is calculated to be 0.96363

Appendix B:
National Presidential Election Results
(1948 - 2004 w/o 1976)
In millions

Table B-1 - National Presidential Election Results
(1948, 1952, 1956,1956, 1960)

Year	1948	1952	1956	1960
Dem	24.179347	27.375090	26.028028	34.220984
Rep	21.991292	34.075529	35.579180	34.108157
Oth	2.622896	0.301323	0.414120	0.503341
Total	48.793535	61.751942	62.021328	68.832482

Source: Leip, David *David Leip's Atlas of U.S. Presidential Elections* (2004), www.uselectionatlas.org

Table B-2 - National Presidential Election Results
(1964, 1968, 1972,1980)

Year	1964	1968	1972	1980
Dem	43.127041	31.271839	29.173222	35.480115
Rep	27.175754	31.783783	47.168710	43.903230
Oth	0.336489	10.144376	1.402095	7.126333
Total	70.639284	73.199998	77.744027	86.509678

Source: Leip, David *David Leip's Atlas of U.S. Presidential Elections* (2004), www.uselectionatlas.org

Table B-3 - National Presidential Election Results
(1984, 1988, 1992,1996)

Year	1984	1988	1992	1996
Dem	37.577352	41.809476	44.909806	47.400125
Rep	54.455472	48.886597	39.104550	39.198755
Oth	0.620409	0.898613	20.409567	9.676521
Total	92.653233	91.594686	104.423923	96.275401

Source: Leip, David *David Leip's Atlas of U.S. Presidential Elections* (2004), www.uselectionatlas.org

Table B-4 - National Presidential Election Results
(2000 & 2004)

Year	2000	2004
Dem	51.003926	59.028439
Rep	50.460110	62.040610
Oth	3.953439	1.224499
Total	105.417475	122.293548

Source: Leip, David *David Leip's Atlas of U.S. Presidential Elections* (2004), www.uselectionatlas.org

References

Apple, R.W., Jr., *New York Times*, (2004). http://www.nytimes.com/ 2004/08/30/politics/campaign/30apple.html

Breipohl, Arthur M. (1970). *Probabilistic Systems Analysis*, John Wiley & Sons, New York.

Business Week (1951). *Business Week.*

Campbell, Angus. (1960). *The American Voter,* University of Chicago Press

Fair, Ray C. (2002). *Predicting Presidential Elections and Other Things*, Stanford University Press

Greenhaven Press's ten book series. (2004). *The Turbulent 60s.*

Gravetter, Frederick J. & Wallnau, Larry B., (1996). *Statistics for the Behavior Sciences, West Publishing*, Fourth Edition, St. Paul, MN.

Leip, David. (2004). *David Leip's Atlas of U.S. Presidential Elections,* http://www.uselectionatlas.org

Library of Congress, *African American Odyssey: The Civil Rights Era* (2004)   http://memory.loc.gov/ammem/aaohtml/exhibit/aopart9.html. Washington, D.C.

Meyers, William P. (2004). *A Brief History of the Democratic Party.*

Moncur, Michael. (2005). *Michael Moncur's (Cynical) Quotations*, http://www.quotationspage.com
Microsoft Corporation. (2005). *Vietnam War, Microsoft® Encarta® Online Encyclopedia 2005.*
http://encarta.msn.com © 1997-2005

Price , Geoff. *Assessing the Vote and the Roots of American Political Divide*. (2004).

http://www.rationalrevolution.net/articles/assessing_the_vote_and_the_r
oots.htm

The National Election Studies, Center for Political Studies, University of Michigan. *The NES Guide to Public Opinion and Electoral Behavior.* (2000) http://www.umich.edu/~nes/nesguide/nesguide.htm. Ann Arbor, MI: University of Michigan, Center for Political Studies [producer and distributor]

U.S. Census Bureau. (2001). *Current Population Survey.*

U.S. Census Bureau. (2002). *Demographic Trends in the 20th Century*

U.S. Census Bureau. (2004-2005). *Statistical Abstract of the United States* (Table No. HS-52)

U.S. Census Bureau. (2004). *Voting & Registration in the November 2004 Election* Online Tables

Index

www.ingramcontent.com/pod-product-compliance
Lightning Source LLC
Chambersburg PA
CBHW031511270326
41930CB00006B/353